Circleway
The Story of the Women's Dream Quest
by
Judith Tripp

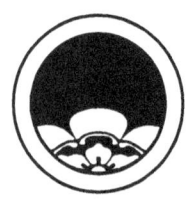

Circleway Press
P.O. Box 1006
Woodacre, CA 94973
www.circleway.com
Copyright 2012 by Judith Tripp
Cover design by Gwyneth Tripp
Cover Image, *Sisiutl*, by Gael Nagel; used with permission

All rights reserved. No part of this book may be reproduced in any form or by any means, electronic or mechanical, including photo-copying recording, or by any information storage and retrieval system without permission in writing from the author.

Printed in 2012

Tripp, Judith, 1948-

Circleway, the Story of the Women's Dream Quest/Judith Tripp, Woodacre, California, Circleway Press

1. Women's Spirituality, 2 Psychology, 3 Soul Work

To my spirit grandmothers, mothers, daughters and granddaughters gathered in the circle of my heart. And to their partners in the sacred dance of creation.

Table of Contents

Prelude...1

What Is the Women's Dream Quest?...3

Creating the Bones...11

Preparing the Temple...35

The Rehearsal...45

Toward the Land of the Soul...73

Intimate Circles in Kairos Time...101

Morning Has Broken...117

The Maiden, Mother, and Crone...131

Tales from Near and Far...161

Growing the Vision...191

Songs...197

Resources...207

About Circleway...209

Hosting a Quest...210

Acknowledgments...211

Prelude

I am early for a meeting at San Francisco's Grace Cathedral to plan our next Women's Dream Quest. I enter into the neo-Gothic sanctuary past Benny Buffano's statue of gentle St. Francis and begin my walk on the path of the 36-foot diameter labyrinth that graces the entrance to the nave. This labyrinth is a replica of the pattern embedded in the floor of Chartres Cathedral in France dating back to 1201. I have walked its curving path hundreds of times over the years. There are no choices along the route, you simply follow the way to the center, pause in meditation and retrace your steps for the outward journey. There is no one else in the cathedral this morning. Sunlight shines through the stunning stained-glass windows and all is quiet and peaceful.

I stand at the entrance to the labyrinth, bow my head in prayer and dedicate this walk to understanding my calling in the world. Slowly, and then with a waltzing rhythm that I have come to trust, I move through the turns, gliding along the long stretches, pivoting in the tight curves. Images of circles of women surrounding this labyrinth flood my mind. I hear Diana's harp. I smell sage. I remember my own voice intoning the rituals we have come to hold dear over the many years of the Quest. I walk on, growing quieter, feeling calm. I sense the presence of the three thousand or so women who have attended these Quests over the years. I have entered the space where we are all connected.

On the inward path of the labyrinth, I let go of my worries. I open to the experience of the walk and anticipate the moment of my entrance into the six-petaled center. How many times I have come to a walk like this, burdened with the issues of my life, and how many times I have felt the burdens slip away as I come to a deeper level of awareness. It is no different today. I find my breath flowing easily, my shoulders relaxing, and a sense of well-being filling me.

As I come to the center, I remember a vision that I had in 1993 of angelic beings dancing on a labyrinth of their own just above me. There is no vision this time, but a definite sense of homecoming. This is a place where I meet my Self. It is a dependable place where I can tune in, heart open and soul deep. I sit on the floor and meditate for a while, holding the question of my calling in the world. Gradually, answers begin to arrive in my consciousness. A strong knowing about my work as a psychotherapist, a workshop leader, a musician. And something new comes: I want to write a book about the Women's Dream Quest.

My outward walk is filled as it often is with ways to implement my visions. How can I make the time to do this writing? What form will this work take? My energy quickens and I fly through the curves and down the long stretches and come to the entrance/exit excited. I feel like I have received one of the sacred assignments of my life.

Chapter One
What Is the Women's Dream Quest?

When the women find their power, no force on earth can stop the flow.

One

Imagine the neo-gothic Grace Cathedral, high on a hill in San Francisco, California, on a Friday night in January, chill and dark, just at the beginning of the new year. One hundred brightly clad women have brought sleeping bags and warm socks and are now sitting down near the baptismal font, singing:

> Come into my Life, Divine Mother
> Hold me in your arms, Divine Mother

Imagine song and dance and psycho-spiritual exercises designed to invite the women to reinhabit their souls. There are twelve small altars scattered over the cathedral floor, each with a theme marking "campsites" for the women. Imagine healing, art, chanting, prayer, and labyrinth walking. Imagine the Women's Dream Quest.

This book tells the story of its flowering and the flowering of a spirituality uniquely suited to our times. It also shares the story of my journey as I have become its shepherd and the journey of the women and men who seek, by practice, word and deed, to restore the sacred feminine to its rightful place in the psyche of Western Civilization.

Our modern world has long undervalued its soulful

imagination. Dominated by mind, power, and commerce, our culture is in short supply of the imaginal, the intuitive, and the truly spiritual.

Imagine the labyrinth at Grace Cathedral's entrance, 36-foot diameter, a path of prayer and meditation where women can walk and take their most tender questions for contemplation. This labyrinth is a replica of the one laid out in stone in the 12th century at Chartres Cathedral in France. People have been walking its spiraling path in search of the Holy for centuries. Its twists and turns soothe the central nervous system and its archetypal pattern contains and tames the flow of thought and feeling that titillates our psyches.

Our world is run on Chronos time, tied to the clock. All of us, children, adults, pets, the chickens in factory farms, are on schedules. We have schedule books, iPhones, Twitter accounts. Days, weeks, even years are planned out by us in advance. We worry about the length of a woman's labor and strain impatiently at the slow pace of death. We hurry and criticize ourselves when we are not productive because we know that time is money.

Imagine a 17-hour event where we are invited to let go of ordinary time and slip into Kairos time, where a moment can last for hours and the whole Quest can take place in the twinkle of an eye. Imagine yourself opening to the idea that we can slow down our breathing and pay attention to the sensations in our bodies, letting go of the mundane and inviting in the sacred.

Our world is ordered by rationality, science, and logic. We shun what we call "superstition," and mistrust feeling and intuition. We form opinions from what we learn in schools, which are becoming devoid of music and art. Liberal Arts education is considered frivolous and technology is worshiped as an end rather than a means.

Imagine an evening where we are encouraged to live in the land of the soul, to drop into another way of being and to leave behind the more confining parts of the mind. Imagine hours of communal singing and praying while walking the labyrinth. Imagine hearts opening to strangers and precious truths told in trust.

Our world is patriarchal. Men's rights in economic, spiritual, and political matters have dominated for centuries. Ironically, the successes of feminism have been measured in terms of how much like men women have become. Both men and women suffer the confining roles the patriarchy has cast in stone.

In place of this patriarchal focus, imagine an evening when the form and content is utterly feminine; where we sit in the circle and honor each one among us regardless of status. Imagine songs and meditations celebrating the feminine face of God. Imagine an event that welcomes all traditions: Christian, Jewish, Pagan, Buddhist, Muslim, and Indigenous. Imagine coming together in a realm where all the spiritual traditions meet beyond the words and concepts that divide us. Imagine the rest and rejuvenation such a realm invites.

Our world tends to listen to the Father's voice. We too often worship only God the Father, elect only men or suitably masculinized women to high public office. We ignore or disparage the gentler, more receptive, often fiercely compassionate qualities of the Mother Voice in either men or women.

Imagine the intention of an evening dedicated to listening to the Mother Voice, giving her time to speak. Imagine numerous opportunities to listen to her and to pray to her.

> Mother, I sing to you,
> Mother I bring you my passion and presence.
> Mother I sing to you,
> Mother, I bring you my life
> Bearing my soul's bright light
> Opening to holy sight,
> Weaving the streams of my life,
> Building the paradise,
> Healing the fear and lies,
> Mother, I gaze through your eyes.

When I first wrote this introduction in Chartres, France,

Easter Monday of 2004, I was far from my familiar space, my California home with its spring-green hills turning a shade golden. I had left behind the daily routines of my long-term psychotherapy practice. Chartres is an archetypal space, a place where the Mother's Voice has never been ignored. I felt her through every moment I spent in the cathedral, in much the way I feel her in the Dream Quest and in these words. I think that she wants us to know her, to hear her call, her distress, her hope for the world. She wants there to be ways for us meet her and ignite the parts of our hearts dedicated to her service. So many have said that her time is at hand, that the imbalance of our planet and our many cultures cry desperately for ways to weave her more consciously and equitably into the tapestry of this world.

Part of my practice in Chartres was to sit in the Mary Chapel each day and listen for her voice. I imagined that she was pleased to have me working on this task. I took comfort and succor from her abiding presence. My prayer for this work is that it will take you to the realms the Quest provides and create a circle for you where you can feel encouraged and where you can receive the healing balm and clarion call of the sacred feminine.

What Happens in a Quest?

Let me begin by giving you a brief rundown: The Quest is a 17-hour workshop where as many as one hundred women gather on a Friday night in Grace Cathedral in San Francisco, California; or in Portland, Oregon; Memphis, Tennessee; Houston, Texas; Seattle, Washington; Kearney, Nebraska; Prince Edward Island, Canada; Charlottesville, Virginia. They bring sleeping bags and personal belongings and stay overnight in the church or retreat center. During those 17 hours, we gather first as a large group, singing, meditating, and participating in a ritual inspired by our theme, which is frequently determined by the season. In the autumn, our Quests are often very introspective in keeping with the darkening season. In the spring, we might focus on the heroine's journey, inspired by the flowering trees. We then break into small groups by randomly choosing a card that represents a medicine animal, a symbolic rune, or a goddess from one of the world's traditions. Everyone who chooses the same card meets together in small groups guided by a therapist or a labyrinth facilitator from the community. The women are encouraged to share their stories, feelings, and wisdom. After an hour of small group time, the participants are free to walk the labyrinth, receive healings and counseling sessions, create dolls or other art, chant with a singer at the high altar, make dream pillows, meditate, or pray somewhere in the church. Healers, artists, massage therapists, and musicians are available to facilitate this part of the evening. The participants are encouraged to sleep when they are ready and to be open to dreaming. We consider anything that happens—dreams, visions, or insights—to be part of the "dream." Our quest is to explore and experience the inner, intuitive side of life.

The next morning, we are awakened very early by a song. The first hour is for silence. Participants journal, record their dreams, meditate, do yoga, or go back to sleep. Then the small groups meet once more for dream sharing and speaking more about the experience of the Quest. At the end of this sharing, we gather as a large group on the labyrinth and move, meditate, and sing together. After we say goodbye to the magical space of the cathedral, we move to the meeting hall for a hearty breakfast. Each group then plans a brief presentation about their experience. We watch each other's presentations, which are sometimes silly, sometimes deep and profound, receive gifts which represent the Quest, and then come together for a final closing ritual. We affirm that our circle is forever and always.

This is a broad overview, but the Quest is so very much more. The following chapters will introduce you to the elements that make up the Quest and the philosophy that guides it.

Chapter Two
Creating the Bones

A great ritual must nod to mystery, hold our longing,
and give us a very good time.

Two

When I began to understand how I create a Quest, I was faced with the knowledge that the ideas for processes, meditations and music seem to "come" to me, sometimes unbidden. If I try to figure out how to achieve a certain effect, it often falls flat. Sometimes it isn't until the day before the event that I integrate just the right combination of music, movement, and drama for the ceremony that will bring just the right combination of mystery, soulfulness, and beauty. I realized that I rely on what the Jungians call the "imaginal" realm of archetypes and deep soul knowing. I access this state of consciousness in my meditations, dreams, music, and movement. In other ages and cultures, the imaginal was considered to be a more important aspect of human consciousness than it is in our rational and technological epoch. In the Quest, we welcome this world of image, poetry, trance, and mystery. We invite the participants to join in. We allow for the soulful thoughts, serendipities, and experiences it engenders.

Let me give you an example of this process: One quest in October actually occurred on Halloween much to the delight of our pagan members. Halloween or Samhein, as it is known in the old religion, is a time of honoring the spirits. The Christian All Saints' Day on November 1 comes from the same desire to relate to those who have died, as do the Day of the Dead celebrations in Mexico and elsewhere. Throughout the Western world during this time in early autumn when the days grow noticeably shorter and cooler, people's thoughts naturally turn inward. People say that on this particular night the veils are most thin between the worlds and that we are more able to experience the presence of those who have died. I have always been intrigued by this idea and by the notion of veils separating this world from the world of spirits. With that thought in mind, the idea for veils hanging from a 40-foot-high balcony in the cathedral arrived when I was participating in a dance on the cliffs of Mendocino. We were using a huge piece of gauze to link the dancers. Suddenly I saw gauzy veils hung from the balcony near the baptismal font in Grace Cathedral. Photographs of deceased loved ones could be attached as though they were watching us through the veils. Women could literally dance between the veils and have a palpable, symbolic experience with their beloved dead.

In the rhythmic pulse of the dance, surrounded by the beauty of the Pacific Ocean and the community of dancers, I had entered into the imaginal realm. I knew that the Quest was coming, I found myself in a meditative state and the idea simply arrived.

This intuitive, "psychic" realm of knowing is familiar to almost all of us. In this realm of consciousness we have our experiences of unity and awareness. We have hunches and flights of fancy. We slip from our everyday minds of analysis and rationality and begin to dream and vision and sense the world we hold as spiritual and sacred. The imaginal realm beckons to Buddhist meditators, rock concert-goers, members of congregations taken with the magic of the mass. It is familiar to people falling in love or holding a newborn baby. To make it explicit and honorable is to change the way the world values such things. In the Quest, we do make it explicit.

I have long trusted the stirrings of the imaginal realm. They have been honed during many experiences in my life and validated by teachers and friends along the way. My childhood gave me ample time to visit this realm.

As often happens to children who live in chaotic environments, I learned early how to rely on my intuition. In order to predict the emotions of my parents, whose moods were many and difficult, I learned to sense what might be coming next. I learned how far I could go in any confrontation with my mother before she would snap into a rage that sent her off into her room with the door slammed. I also retreated into another realm when the world of my parents and their problems were too difficult for me to handle emotionally.

At age 3, I had an elaborate relationship with an imaginary friend who lived behind a flower on the 1950s wallpaper of my living room. I remember loving him and his family very much. But as happened too often in my family, my parents began taking up the story, inviting him to dinner, sighting him in his red MG (my father's favorite car). I can remember humoring them, playing along with the story, even appreciating their loving intentions, but I knew that they were not seeing him. My own experience was distinct and belonged to another realm to which they had no access. This is one of my earliest memories. At age 4 or 5, I let my friend go. However, some part of that realm still remained alive in my childhood, transferred to beloved dolls and a plastic blue bird I held dear. My father encouraged my imagination and gave me a great gift by playing with me in the elaborate world we constructed in my room with characters I remember to this day.

In my forties, I had a psychic reading that introduced me to a guide from the realm of the Ascended Masters. I immediately recognized my old friend. He stood in long robes, his white hair thick and curling. He had a beautiful, kind face and gentle bearing. The same feeling from my earlier imaginal experiences with him reentered my life and gave me a sense of affirmation that he had, indeed, been with me throughout my life. I have since used his presence as a conduit for relating to the imaginal realm. In my "conversations" with him, his voice is a constant, reasonable one. Sometimes I open my mind, picturing his kindly face and letting words come to me. I have journals of these conversations that always shed an objective and wise light on a particular issue I may be dealing with. These conversations are healing in the sense that I have an ongoing relationship with a male figure who seems to have always been with me, kind and protective, occasionally challenging me, but always with my highest good in mind. In Jungian terms, he is my animus.

In the imaginal realm, the presence of guides, angels, animal totems, divine presences, and voices are common and natural things. In the Quest, women sometimes dream of angels or find themselves attracted to certain animals or goddesses. Sometimes they will know their totem animal from an experience with a shaman or sense the presence of their guardian angel walking beside them on the labyrinth. Many people experience a wise voice whispering in their ear as they stand in the circle or walk the labyrinth. During the Quest we all seek to open up to the possibility of this kind of conversation and inspiration. Our modern minds are hungry for metaphor, and most all of us are able to access a guiding or protecting image. Often our dreams are the source of such figures, and in the Quest we encourage all kinds of dreams.

Bringing it to Earth

After I have received the initial idea for the Quest theme, it is time for me to call the circle. I email the list leaders—therapists, artists, spiritual teachers—who have been involved with the Quest since the beginning. Out of a pool of twenty or more women, ten to twelve choose to participate as small group leaders. It is always interesting to see who comes to a particular Quest. The whole experience is colored and shaped by the unique hearts of the leaders. I always know that there will be movement and poetry when Clover is a small group leader and that we will have a thorough-going investigation of the animal totem when Riki leads. The leaders have the important task of providing a safe circle for the women in their small group. They ponder the theme and take responsibility for guiding the experience of the individual participants through attentive listening, creation of safety and acceptance, and generally filling their individual circles with loving kindness.

My next step is to choose the archetypal energies that we will call upon to guide us during the Quest. These include either Jamie Sam's wonderful animal medicine cards, the Runes of Richard Bloom, or a set of cards depicting goddesses from different traditions and times. I will draw a card for each group leader and make eight copies of it for her. Then at the Quest, each of the participants will draw a card to determine her small group. In the fall, I like to use the animal cards. Since the fall is associated with the Crone aspect of the goddess in the Pagan tradition, and because the crone is often associated with her animal familiars, it seems fitting to invoke the gifts and qualities of the animals. In the spring Quests, since there is often a dreamier, youthful quality to the season, the more abstract runes seem fitting as our guides. From time to time, particularly when we focus particularly on the sacred feminine, we use the goddess cards.

Regardless of what symbols or images we use, what seems most important is to call on help from the imaginal world. The animal cards are a strong conduit for energies between the worlds. Familiar and symbolic, they immediately conjure up meaning when people look at them. Everyone relates to the ferocity of the mountain lion, the shyness of the deer, the stealth of the weasel. Jamie's compilation of Indian traditional lore about the animals adds more to these initial impressions and points the way to the symbolic teachings that are associated with each animal.

On the other hand, the runes mark different moments in the spiritual journey, for example, opening, stillness, breakthrough. Ralph Bloom has created a set of symbolic runes from ancient norse mythology. They look like ,"//" or ">", and are presented on small stones. They offer us an opportunity to reflect on our current place on the path. The serendipity of choosing just the right rune brings a nudge to the woman choosing it, asking her to examine her current process.

When we use the goddess cards, another dimension of the sacred feminine is brought forth. I like to think of the sacred feminine as both particle and wave. The waves are the qualities of receptivity, fierce compassion, interconnectedness, yielding, etc. that are attributed to the yin side of our psyches. The particles are the different goddesses who have been worshiped throughout time and in every culture. Images of Inanna, Isis, Demeter, Freya, Bridget,

Mary, Quan Yin, and Shechinah are powerful reminders of the feminine face of God. In Quests where we have invited these goddesses, women are drawn to the beauty and power of the sacred feminine throughout time and culture.

I make a ceremony for choosing the cards or runes. In my woodland studio, I light a candle, tune into my breath, and begin to hold the Quest and its theme in my mind. I inwardly call to the women who will be participating as small group leaders, and the unknown women who will be participants, thus initiating the first circle of this particular Quest. I ask for the blessings of Mother-Father God and all beings for whom the Quest is offered. Gazing at the cards, which I have spread face down on my small wooden labyrinth, I inwardly ask which animals would like to come and be with us in this Quest. Then I randomly select the ten cards to which my hand feels drawn. This time Bear appears and Turkey (always a challenge), Dragonfly, Eagle, Hawk, Grouse, Spider, Snake, Swan, and Elk. As I draw Fox for myself. I reflect on how the fox medicine will play out in my life during the weeks of preparation before the Quest. Yes, I think, I have some political situations in my life that might benefit from skillful, stealthy consideration.

Once I have elected this group of ten cards, I think of each small group leader, one by one. I imagine her and all I know about her path and what is transpiring in her life at the moment, and then randomly pick a card for her. Almost always the card fits the small group leader. After I have reported the results of this ceremony, I get emails from them. Maia tells me that she contemplates embracing her grace when she receives Swan. Patty receives Turkey and ponders the boundaries of giving. Karen joyfully receives Eagle for a second time and takes its appearance in her life as a beacon toward power and spiritual clarity. Here is what Riki has to say about her card:

> When I receive my card, I tune into my first impressions, sit with them and whether I like the card or not, I feel launched. I read the description of this animal in the Animal Cards book and pull the color card from my deck and make an altar with candles to start it off. I look at the card and wait for other objects to come to mind so that the connection to this animal will become more visible and conscious.
>
> I let go for a while, being amazed and delighted by how this animal soon takes over my life! When I received the mouse, I laughed and yelled because I was struggling with a mouse that had moved into my kitchen and I had tried many kinds of safe traps and even put her outside but she kept coming back. Now the spirit of the animal would finally get me to listen, I was annoyed and delighted. I watched the mouse with curiosity and imagined the life of mice from this lived-with experience. Mouse talked to me in my dreams and I finally allowed myself to feel what (with newfound cleverness and quickness) I had never been able to integrate personally before.
>
> I read Native American writings about this animal,

everything I can and then any information from any other indigenous cultures I can find. I also read myths and stories with these animals as characters.

And then I ask for the animal to show me what more I need to know for this group that will be coming. I watch my dreams for any connections to the animal. I enjoy how the animal shows up EVERYWHERE, suddenly like a practical joke between me and the ancestors, the larger collective unconscious that is now more accessible for learning and deepening my awareness of this layer of our existence we're not always tuned into.

Each of the small group leaders will use her animal as an object of contemplation over the coming weeks. She will meditate on the qualities of the animal and begin to choose objects for an altar she will make on the cathedral floor. This altar will welcome her group to their place in the cathedral. She will color the set of eight cards with the outline of the animal's image and inwardly call on the people who will be coming into her small group. Rafts of Turkey feathers will come Patty's way, and Ann will find elk skin medicine bags in an obscure catalogue and order enough for her group. The Quest begins in earnest during this activity of coloring cards and creating beautiful altars.

There is something primordially maternal about the process, as if we are making a cozy nest to shelter those who will come to sing, dream, and walk the labyrinth. Time after time I am astounded at the creativity that is unleashed by suggesting that a woman make a symbolic altar. When we gather in the conference room at the cathedral before the Quest, flowers, fabulous cloths, pieces of art depicting the group's theme and thoughtful gifts for each of the participants fill the room. I remember one altar created for Quan Yin in a Quest that we dedicated to the goddesses of all traditions. The altar cloth was a white antique table cloth designed in the shape of the petals of a flower. In the center of the petals there was a leafy green plant that formed the backdrop for a seated Quan Yin statue. There were votive candles arranged randomly over the cloth and a lacy white fan waiting to serve as the "talking stick." We all seem drawn to decorating the temple. We use our sense of beauty to pay homage to the sacred and to the participants we serve.

  This mindful and creative preparation allows all of the small group leaders to enter into the imaginal realm. Someone always thanks me for giving her the opportunity to leave some demanding workday task behind in order to buy the flowers for the altar or take on the job of coloring the cards. It gives her an opportunity to slow down and receive the blessing of relaxation and grace that comes from entering into this realm. Each of the small group leaders is asked to meditate on the theme and to sort out their own experiences and feelings around it. They are asked to pay attention to their feelings and associations with the animal card they have received. For this Halloween Quest, they will meditate on their own ancestors and on loved ones or family who have passed away. They will contemplate their relationship to death and how they feel about helping others encounter their own reactions to the deaths of loved ones. The small group leaders pay attention to their dreams and notice what they are writing in their journals and what they are thinking about. They open themselves up to the possibility that the Quest may be providing a theme for their own lives, as well as the lives of the participants. It is essential that we all feel that the Quest is meaningful and important to us personally. I have found that the Quests are always a chance to come more deeply into my own process. My circle was surprised that I wanted to lead the week after my beloved father's passing. I could think of no place that I would rather be. I felt closer to him and more in touch with my feelings while doing my work and participating in the circle we created than I would have felt on my own. My friend Crystal, who had been my co-leader for many years of the Quest, returned to support me and we carried on.

    The small group leaders of the Portland Quest have made a year-round circle based on the Quest. They come together in the spring to randomly select their card from the list of the animals I have drawn for their quest. They make a study of the effect of the animal on their day-to-day life throughout the year. When the Quest comes in January, they are deeply immersed in the archetype their animal inspires. This year, Peg, who has been one of the "mothers" of the Portland Quest is dealing with a tragic health problem in her family. Peg has had a history drawing large land animals as her totems. I can remember one year when she got a dragonfly and was delighted to pursue the air element for a change. She felt that drawing this animal indicated that she was taking life more lightheartedly. This year, she told me, she was praying for a return to the large, dependable Elk or Buffalo to help guide her through the next months. She was surprised when she drew her card in August. Black Panther arrived to help her during these months—an animal of power and grace that could inspire her own fierce strength.

My other preparation for the Quest experience involves walking the labyrinth several times in Grace Cathedral, but also the seven-circuit medieval labyrinth in the drive in front of my home. This helps me to tune into my guidance about what needs to happen in the Quest. Turning in a prayerful way to the Mother, I walk to experience clarity from the inner realms. Often an idea like the one for the veils happens, other times a validation for what we are attempting to invoke this time around. Most often, the walk is a communion with the inner guidance that I rely on to direct me in all of this work. There has been a continuity in this inner relationship during all of these years. When I enter this state of consciousness, I am a scribe, a conduit for spiritual inspiration. I feel expanded and attuned at the end of these walks. I emerge with practical, feasible tasks, fortified to do the work. I cannot imagine creating the Quest without this practice.

I remember back in 2010 as I was preparing for the second Ancestor Quest, I heard a news story about Barack Obama and George W. Bush being distantly related. Someone had done the research into their genealogy and found them to be distant cousins. I cannot imagine two more different souls and yet, in the realm of blood and genetics, their kinship came to life. I have also been fascinated by the accounts that all of us on the planet come from only four distinct genetic groups. When I walked the labyrinth with the Ancestor theme in mind, I fell into a meditation where I saw the circles of the ancestors arrayed behind me, connected by family lines that converged many generations back. I saw a giant web with glistening strands connecting the individual ancestors, some through a spiritual lineage, some across familial ties. It seemed to me that the ancestors might know that we are all connected, not fractured bits of cultural and political groupings. With these thoughts and the vision of the meditation in mind, I sat down with my guitar and came up with a song that asked:

> When will we remember our one true blood
> That flows in every vein?
> When will we remember our one true blood
> And build our family again?
> When will we remember the ancestors' web
> That lives in every mind
> And know your kin are mine?

After I got that far, thinking of the blood that connects us and the concepts that could remind us of the truth below the surface of ideologies and prejudices, I thought about the heart and wrote:

> When will we remember the one true heart
> That beats in every breast?
> When will we remember the one true heart
> And leave the wars at last?

The Labyrinth

I have known about the Chartres labyrinth since 1992 when Rev. Dr. Lauren Artress first told a group of us who had been working with the Dream Quest and other outreach ministries at Grace Cathedral about a wonderful meditation tool that she had discovered while working with Dr. Jean Houston, noted psychologist and philosopher. This tool was a pattern found in the floor of Chartres Cathedral in France. Part of the Christian tradition, it had been laid in the stone floor of the cathedral in 1201 as a symbol of the path to the holy land. It was intended for pilgrims who were unable to reach Jerusalem during the crusades. At the time, several cathedrals in northern France had been designated as pilgrimage sites where pilgrims could fulfill their obligation

Lauren details her first walk in Chartres in her book, *Walking a Sacred Path*. This involved removing the cathedral chairs that normally cover the 42-foot diameter pattern and beginning a long and interesting relationship with the church officials in Chartres. Lauren felt called in her own spiritual journey to revive this archetypal pattern and as she says, pepper the planet with labyrinths. In the twenty some years now since her initial exploration, thousands of new labyrinths have been created all over the world as the result of her calling and the success of her book, now printed in several languages. These join the ages-old labyrinths carved into stone walls, set with stones on cliffs overlooking the sea, and hidden in places of power in nearly every culture on the planet.

Today people walk labyrinths in churches, hospitals, prisons, schools and parks and report sensations of relaxation, peace, meditative calm and inspiration. Its pattern is attractive to people in all segments of society. Nearly everyone who takes the twenty-to-forty-minute journey begins to breathe more easily. Sometimes they find an answer to a disturbing question, and sometimes they experience a deep spiritual feeling of homecoming.

I see the labyrinth as a ground of being inscribed with a path that gives context to the joys and struggles of life. It diagrams the possibilities of turning and returning again, of trusting the path to take us home and of containing the ebbs and flows of life's experiences. It teaches about relationship; about encountering, passing, being passed by others and about meeting another person at the edge or in the center of life.

The walk is threefold. The impulse to go in, let go, perhaps ask a question is one experience. The stillness in the center and what transpires in the realm of contemplation is the second. Finally, the outward journey helps to digest the experience of receiving guidance in the center and gives us the opportunity to see how to put the inner counsel we receive into action. For example, I can enter the labyrinth with a question about how to create a dance that represents the ancestors. I may feel agitated or unsettled and without a clear idea of what I want to do. During the walk, I shed my agitation and return to a more simple state. By the time I get to the center and sit down in meditation, I am open to receive an inspiration. My inner vision turns on and I see how using the entire cathedral as our stage for honoring the ancestors would work. When I feel ready for the return walk, I begin to plan the logistical pieces that will actualize the vision. I think, *we can place tables near the labyrinth filled with candles*. The participants can take one after they are led through the veils. There will be a drum beating a heartbeat as we walk. Eureka!

Walking the labyrinth is a practice we do with our whole body. As we walk its sinuous path, our central nervous system is stimulated and balanced by the pattern of the turns. The mind is quieted by the mantra of the feet. As we come to know the experience as a practice, so too do we use it like a meditation cushion or a rosary, as a way of letting our souls know that we are ready to listen and perhaps to pray.

The labyrinth is like a womb. It incubates our dreams and yearnings. It is a guiding practice, a container for whatever feeling, sensation, opinion, or vision we have during our relationship with it. Because the walk has a duration and a familiar form, it invites our psyche to relax into the knowledge that we can return again and again. Because it is beautiful and round, has six symbolic petals, and has history, the labyrinth gives our busy minds something to chew on.

Now these are all analytical impressions of the labyrinth. To the medieval pilgrims and to the ancients who may have first created the pattern, the labyrinth simply was a pattern that human beings make like bees knowing to make hexagonal containers for their honey. Like the other familiar symbols in the church, it was a signal to the spirit, to honor and attend to the inner journey itself.

To me, the Chartres labyrinth is a beacon from the 12th century mind and spirit. There are many opinions among scholars about its origin and purpose. However, it is clear that the labyrinth was an intentional design. Perhaps it was created by those who kept alive the teachings of the ancient mystery schools. Perhaps the imaginal realms were more accessible and honored in the 12th century and this labyrinth was a device for opening the individual to the experience of God. In the cathedral, the labyrinth lies at the opening of the sanctuary. When you walk it, you are surrounded by the glories of the cathedral. As you enter the center, you face the high altar, the place of the sacrament, where you are invited to partake of the body and blood of Christ. You have been twisted and turned, confronted possibly, by the current stories in your mind. You come to the center and there is an implicit invitation to go deeper into the sacred realm. Our 21st century body/minds respond to the invitation just like our ancient kin. Hungry as I believe we are for the experience of the sacred accorded through the imaginal realm, we use the labyrinth to enter the kingdom, to access sacred feminine intuition, to experience an arrival in the Tao, to find oneself in the Holy of Holies. Depending on our tradition, the labyrinth complies with this centering metaphor. It does not require a particular story or dogma to work its magic.

The 12th century in Chartres was filled with the everyday experience of the story of the Bible. The cathedral is full of characters from the old and new testaments in stone and glass and painting. A pilgrim of the time would be surrounded by life-size figures of prophets and saints, painted to be life-like. It would be unlike anything he had ever seen before. He would know that he was standing in a place where the relic of the Virgin's veil had miraculously been saved from a great fire and that everyone in the region had banded together to rebuild Her cathedral in even greater grandeur. He would know that artisans and masons and architects had, in a frenzy of construction, completed the heavenly building in 30 years. He would have heard the legend that the quarry workers worked in silent prayer. He would know that the artisans sang hymns as they worked. Everything about the place, including its labyrinth was designed to take him to heaven.

I believe that the energetic trace of this reality lives in the Chartres labyrinth. Whenever I walk it, I feel the grace of that long-ago time—perhaps more innocent than ours—certainly more amenable to the simple sublime story of Christianity and a story where the sacred feminine has a particular, honored role. The many replicas of the Chartres labyrinth now all over the world carry something of this spirit with them.

When those of us who have been moved by the labyrinth find our way to Chartres, we encounter the 12th century experience writ large. Called by the labyrinth, we may find our way to Mary, whose home Chartres is. I know I did and that this connection, for me, is vital. I will never forget the morning that my friend Alyssa took me by the hand and led me to the chapel of Our Lady of the Pillar, the 15th century Black Madonna statue that rests on top of a 6-foot pillar. As I sat down, every part of my body relaxed and I felt like I had come home. A sweet and gentle feeling of being loved filled me. I have found my way to this chapel every time I have visited Chartres. I light a candle, sit in meditation and wait for an internal message that has never failed to come. When I stayed in Chartres for my sabbatical, I "heard" her say, "Let me heal you with my Grace, I am your constant mother." She has become my constant mother. Whenever I walk a labyrinth part of me revisits that chapel.

So walking the labyrinth in preparation for the Quest carries with it this trail of experience. Stepping on its path connects me with the lineage of Mary, connects me with Chartres, my spiritual home, and also connects me with the experiences of all the other labyrinth walks I have participated in and with all the walkers and Questers. I like to think that this web of connections inspires me to create just what is needed for a particular Quest.

The imaginal realm also knocks on my door at odd times during the weeks of preparation. Occasionally, I will have a dream about the Quest, or a reflection in the middle of a ferry ride to San Francisco. For example, here is an excerpt from my journal, written before the Halloween Quest:

> This Quest is about creating a safe container for the encounter with the world of the dead. It has the wild and wooly aspect of Halloween and all of the concepts that go with it. Your job is to ride that high energy to the land of the soul, which is, of course, the larger unseen world. Make sure you allow plenty of room for grounding and for quiet inner solitude. It is always a choice to tune in to the other beings/spirits, and we each have a unique relationship with these beings.

I listen to this inner voice and take in the instructions. I think about my beliefs about the afterlife and communication with the dead. This message of guidance becomes one voice in an inner conference about how to create the Quest. I like to integrate the practical and theoretical knowledge of my left-brained voice with the imaginal voice. I know that one of the tenets of the Quest is to welcome women holding various metaphysical beliefs. What I want to engender in this feminine-based spirituality is a tolerance for difference and a celebration of diversity. If we are able to make invitations and suggestions rather than authoritative dogma, we stand a chance of meeting in a heartful space.

I find myself in a partnership with the imaginal realm that fosters a marriage of the seen and unseen, the sacred and secular, the masculine and feminine. When held in mutual respect, the forces that are at odds in the patriarchy can come to a partnership in the new ways we are creating.

Chapter Three
Preparing the Temple

We bring the flowers, light the candles and join our opened hearts with the ages-old splendor of the cathedral. Sacred Space arrives.

Three

On the day of the Quest, I sleep in as long as I can until the excitement of the day awakens me. I know that I will be up late tonight and that all of my energy will be needed to help lift us into the sacred realms. I go about my morning routines of yoga and a walk with my golden retriever. I take time to pray for grace and ease in the Quest. I begin to load the car with the things that have been accumulating in my hallway. Usually there are many things to pack up: sheets, a pillow, a warm quilt, and my Therm-a-Rest pad with its insulation, which is great for the cold cathedral floor. I take my guitar and flute, tingsha bells, CDs, and booklets. There is a gift for the small group leaders and for each of the participants. This year it is a spherical bell worn as a pendant. It comes in a beautiful Chinese box. I think of it as a way to call the ancestors. It caught my eye in the middle of a catalog of party favors and trinkets. It is truly beautiful and something I am sure the women will wear as a keepsake of the Quest.

I load up the beautiful clothes I have selected. One of the hidden benefits of the Quest is the excuse to buy lovely, flowing dresses, shawls, and robes. I select an outfit that holds the colors of the season, a moss-green dress with a shawl of embroidered and beaded flowers. I will wear the necklace that my spiritual brother, Frank, designed after a dream image he had of me conducting a ceremony and wearing this piece. My dog and cat begin to look restless. It definitely looks like I am going on a trip and they are never happy about that. I check my email, answer a few last minute calls and begin the hour-long trip to Grace Cathedral, exhilarated and happy.

One year at the October Quest, California had held on to her summer until that very day. I was disappointed that it was so warm. The Crone Quest needs a stormy night for proper atmosphere and all my injunctions to let go into the welcoming darkness would be out of place with an 80-degree evening in store for us. Happily the season changed on a dime. Rain clouds, which are truly a blessed event during California Octobers, appeared, and by the time I reached the Waldo Grade, a high hill just before the Golden Gate bridge, there were actual piles of hail beside the road! It was cold and crisp, absolutely the perfect climate for hunkering down for the Autumn Quest.

At the cathedral, I set up the room that the small group leaders will meet in. I make a centerpiece with a cloth and a candle. I arrange the four small Japanese tea cups that always hold our anointing water and fill them with water I have brought back from the Chalice Well in Glastonbury, England. This water is world renowned for its healing powers, rising as it does from the land of ancient Avalon. I arrange the handouts and parking vouchers at each place. I play my flute and invite the spirit to fill the room with goodness and love. I sit then and ground myself in breath and prayer.

It seems to me that each of these acts is part of what makes the Quest work. The small group leaders will be hurrying to the cathedral. If they are welcomed by peace and calm and beauty, they will immediately find their own centers and be ready for our work. There is a cascading effect to the peace and calm and beauty; it enters the whole of the Quest from here. We are all within the safety of the circle and if we all feel cared for, we will be able and willing to care for the circle of participants.

Soon Aisha, our volunteer coordinator, arrives with a carload of food, pumpkins, and harvest decorations. She will organize seven or so volunteers who trade their labor for coming to the event, to set up for registration, arrange food, and set up tables, chairs, and art stations. We hug hello, and check in with each other. I remind her to be sure to create a circle with her volunteers by sitting together for a few minutes to breathe and check in with one another. We do this so that the same care touches everyone who is working on the event.

At about 2 p.m., the small group leaders begin arriving with armloads of flowers and baskets overflowing with what one woman calls her spiritual tchotchkes. It has been a while since we have all seen each other so the room fills with the warm chatter of friends catching up. Although the schedule says that we begin at 2 p.m., it is usually 2:45 before we begin our first circle.

I ask everyone to begin to enter the land of the soul. We breathe and sigh, sometimes groan our way into the silence, sensing our circle complete and ready one more time. I lead the women in a meditation very similar to the one I will use with the whole group later on in the evening. We are all longtime meditators and we easily begin to deepen our breathing together and settle into a contemplative space. We attend to the body, asking it to let go of the stress of getting here. We send a breath to tight shoulders and clenched jaws, exhaling the tension, breathing in relaxation. We visualize the circle we form and remember the leaders who have come to other Quests. We imagine with all the love of kindly angels the women who will put themselves into our care for the evening. This day we also remember the beloved ones who have passed. We call them into our midst, ask their guidance for the All Hallows' Eve Quest and see if there are any special messages any of us need to receive from this realm. I think of my father who died the previous year. My breath deepens and I feel his abiding presence. I sing:

> Ancestors calling, calling tonight.
> Ancestors calling our spirits to flight
> Come join the dance of the great round of life
> Come join us dancing on this sacred night.
> Dancing, dancing, come join the dance of all life
> Dancing, dancing, come join the dancing tonight.

I sense that everyone has gone deeply into the land of the soul. We have visualized together and prayed for the success of our Quest. We have made room for the feelings and sensations, worries and joys of each woman, allowing these things to come to her consciousness. Now it is time to share with each other how we feel. Using a sacred beanbag, the veteran of many circles, as our "talking stick" we go around the circle sharing about the state of our lives, the meaning that the animal card has brought to us, the things we are afraid of or overjoyed about.

One woman shares that she has fallen in love, another has lost her father. Still another finds that having that grouse card has been a harbinger of coming to terms with the chaos of her life. As we go around the circle, tears well up in our eyes over one woman's hard work in her own therapy and giggles erupt over the antics of Patty's newly adopted sons. By the time we have circled the table, we feel like we have been together for ages. We give advice to a woman on her first solo as a small group leader and hold hands in the first of many benedictions.

After going over the logistics for the Quest, which this year includes a new dance through the veils and figuring out how to attach the photocopied photos of loved ones that will be part of the ritual, we go up into the cathedral to claim our spots for the night. Since the cathedral is open to the public until 6 p.m., we can only scope out the spots we will claim for our groups. We do this stealthily since we do not want to disturb the busy daytime life of cathedral visitors. After each leader has found a spot, we meet at the baptismal font, which is on a pedestal near the entrance to the labyrinth, to prepare for our first walk. We hold hands in the circle. I ask that we take this walk together solely for our own benefit. This Quest is about our own renewal and respite as well as that of the participants. At this moment we are still in our ordinary clothes and look like the other cathedral visitors. We line up at the entrance to the labyrinth and one by one begin our walk. This time we have the labyrinth to ourselves and within a few moments we are all on some part of the 36-foot diameter path.

This is one of my favorite parts of the Quest. Everything is set in motion and the momentum of our memories of being in this space so many times before begins to carry us. I look around the circle at my friends and cherish the moments we are all on our path together. As the walk begins, our solo dancer Thais and her little daughter appear. Diana and Portia, our harpists, join us. All of these women love to dance, and they glide on the labyrinth using their arms to make beautiful sweeping and prayerful gestures. Hugs are given along the way along with simple bows of acknowledgment. Often I see tears of relief and homecoming, and tender smiles of recognition.

After the walk, we reassemble at the font. Using the holy water we go around the circle and anoint each other, giving a blessing for a good Quest. This often draws the attention of people in the cathedral. One year in the spring, we had an omen of things to come.

As we were gathering, with about half of the women still on the labyrinth, a young couple came up to the font to join us. They stayed even as more and more of the small group leaders appeared. When we were all there, I explained to them what we were doing and asked if they would like to join us. I asked the young man in particular if he would be willing to stand in for his whole gender. With giggles, they agreed and participated in the blessing. As providence would have it, the young man blessed my forehead and wished me well in the Quest. What beautiful, sincere eyes he had! When we talked about this later, several of us commented that this was the sign we had been waiting for that it was time for there to be a Dream Quest for men and women together.

Now it is time for dinner and changing into our priestess garb. All the small group leaders, dancers, and musicians are here by now and we enjoy the supper that Aisha and her volunteers have provided for us. When 6 p.m. arrives, we make the mad dash for the cathedral and set up altars and this year the veils. Cindy and Dawn valiantly struggle to hang 40-foot lengths of netting from the balcony of the mezzanine. Photos from the small group leaders already adorn the higher reaches. I see my parents, my Dusty dog, grandmothers, soldiers, and tender babies, along with the faces of famous beloved people. It is an awesome sight in the darkening cathedral. There are spaces to walk between the veils, a sense of the imaginal "other side" clearly demarcated in physical space.

The small group leaders go about their tasks of creating unique and beautiful altars with lighted candles that look like campfires around the cathedral. Diana and Portia tune their harps, and I set up my instruments and stake out my sleeping place by the Notre Dame de la Belle Verriere, a replica of the beautiful blue Mary window in Chartres. There is a flurry of activity setting up the art tables and making sure we understand how to operate the lights. I go around the cathedral looking at the beautiful altars. Ten different spaces have been transformed into beautiful depictions of the animal spirits. Vases of fresh flowers, candles, little gifts, and inventive talking sticks adorn each circle. The small group leaders stand proudly by their creations, anticipating the Quest.

I go to the center of the labyrinth with Diana and a volunteer who happens by. We pray for a good Quest, that the women who come will be nourished and cared for and that we too will be challenged and nurtured. We pray that the good work we do will go on out into the world and continue throughout all time.

All of these steps are the necessary ingredients for the beginning of the Quest. I send my intentions soaring upward toward the cathedral vaults, asking that we foster love and open-heartedness, asking that the spirits help to create safety as well as wonder.

Chapter Four
The Rehearsal

Row, Row, Row your Boat,
Gently down the Stream
Merrily, Merrily, Merrily, Merrily
Life is but a Dream

Four

Then, it is time. We call for the participants who have been gathering in the basement level of the cathedral. They come up the stairs carrying their gear, duffle bags, teddy bears, sleeping bags, blowup mattresses, and blankets. They stash their gear in the side aisle and then some of the women have been here before take their usual places by the font. Others take in the cathedral's majesty and their faces look tenuous and a bit afraid. The small group leaders are hostesses and they encourage the women to sit down and sing with me. Diana and Portia have set up their harps next to the font behind me, and I take up my guitar as we launch into the first song of every Dream Quest:

> Row, row, row your boat
> Gently down the stream
> Merrily, merrily, merrily, merrily
> Life is but a dream.

With this incantation, we begin our journey in a lighthearted but profound way. We remember how easy it is to sing a round and offer our voices up to an instant harmony. We remind ourselves that the dreamtime is near and that we can enter it at will to explore it—merrily. Implicit in this song are our experiences of childhood, when song and play were perhaps closer at hand. With the last phrase, we introduce the idea that everything that is about to happen is a dream. All of the insights, visions, experiences in the group rituals and individual epiphanies as well as the nighttime dreams are part of the dream that we are questing.

We then begin to focus on "arriving" to the Quest—leaving the workaday world behind, remembering to breathe and call ourselves into the moment with body, mind, and soul. We sing:

> Earth my body,
> Water, my blood,
> Air, my breath
> And fire, my spirit!

We stand rooted, knees slightly bent, breathing deeply into our bodies. We gesture toward the Earth, remembering our grounding and solidity. Then we move our arms and torsos in a wave-like motion, remembering the watery nature of our bodies, our blood and lymph, our tears. Next we tune into the air that flows into our lungs and then travels as oxygen through all of the cells of our bodies. Finally, we remember the metaphoric fire that animates us by taking a step forward and clapping our hands in a gesture like a shooting arrow.

This part of the song reminds us of our likeness to the world around us, how we are composed elementally of the same as the stuff as the planet—no different on this level than the trees, creatures, clouds, and volcanoes. We evoke the gestures of long-ago camp songs because the body gets this principle of similarity much more readily than our conditioned minds.

Antiphonally layered on top of this pagan chant by Starhawk, we add a fragment of a lovely song by Ferron:

> By my life, be I spirit
>
> By my heart, be I woman
>
> By my eyes, be I open
>
> And by my hands, be I whole

Again, we gesture, breathing in the beautiful words through the body, stretching, touching the heart, gesturing to our eyes to indicate their openness and seeing our working hands, so essential in the manifestation of our spiritual ideals. We recall that by living here on earth, simply by being born, we bring spirit into matter. Our very lives in their complex manifestation are the stuff of heaven as well as of the earth. We affirm the special gifts we carry as women. We acknowledge the gift of sight and through that seeing the possibility of our openness to compassion and acceptance. And then comes the beautiful line that speaks of action. Our wholeness comes from using our hands in the world. It is by our hands that we can touch and create. This is what makes us whole.

I have learned the lesson of that line in my life. While presenting at a seminar in Chartres in May 2007, I blithely began to descend a set of slippery steps into a garden at the ancient seminary next to the cathedral. I fell backward and landed on my wrists, breaking both of them. I have been unraveling the meaning thread of this accident for a while now. My wholeness slowly returned when I regained the use of my hands after a summer of healing. The time I spent as the handless maiden was so very much a meditation on being. I know that I will never take for granted the incredible gift we have of having hands that complete our intentions. They feed and clean us and do a million practical things. For me, they play the flute and guitar and gesture expressively during my counseling sessions. As my right animus hand gradually retrieved the ability to touch, heal, play my instruments, and support me in the downward dog yoga position, I have learned bone deep about the precious wholeness of hands.

In these few lines, we acknowledge our spiritual nature, our feminine hearts, our willingness to be open and our dedication to practice. When these two songs are sung together, it is at first great fun to hear how they magically harmonize, but then the meaning begins to sink in and we feel the stage being set for the rest of the Quest. Our object is to remember our roots, our embodied presence married to the principle of spiritual action. As with "Row, Row, Row Your Boat," this song gives women the ability to experience the harmony of music and gesture. As the great teacher Marion

Woodman says, "the soul is manifest in the body." These songs remind us of that truth.

About this time, I remind everyone that we are merely rehearsing for the Dream Quest and that after the rehearsal, we will begin the actual ritual. In some fundamental way, of course, we have already begun, but saying this allows for the observers among us to be satisfied that they aren't somehow already in the middle of a ritual. It gives us the opportunity to know that there is a difference between the usual Chronos time and the Kairos time of ritual. In Chronos time, we are ruled by clocks, calendars, and our chronological ages; in Kairos, a day may go by in an instant, a Dream Quest may feel like weeks. In Kairos, we can be 10 years old or 90. And most importantly, the tyranny of the orderly mind is suspended and we relax and dream.

Next comes "Return Again" by Schlomo Carlebach:

> Return again, return again,
>
> Return to the land of the soul.
>
> Return to who you are,
>
> Return to what you are,
>
> Return to where you are,
>
> Born and reborn again.

This song gave me words for a way of conceptualizing the

difference between the sacred and ordinary. In the Quest, we make the journey between the two a conscious act. We can think of the sacred as another entire landscape. We can make a decision to return to it again and again. It seems to be in the nature of human beings to drift away from the sacred realm. We seem to lose the thread of spiritual intention and return to the land of the ordinary, forgetting about the Big Mind that mediates our experience in the expanded consciousness of spiritual life.

In the Quest, we draw awareness to the two worlds and create experiences that allow for easy travel between them. Accessing the imaginal realm through mindfulness practices gives us the tools we need to enter the land of the soul at will.

People experience the land of the soul in many and various ways. Each spiritual tradition has methods of meditation and prayer which invite this journey. It does take a change of consciousness to enter this land. Being in nature can move us with beauty and overtake the usual chatter in the mind. We can enter the land of the soul in prayer or meditation. We can dance or chant our way in. In the Quest we use a variety of different techniques to make the invitation, all of which draw our awareness to the inner, watching experience.

During my retreat in Chartres, the distinction between the two lands became very clear. Even the structure of the cathedral building helped make the point. When you enter the cathedral you come into a small vestibule before you actually enter the sanctuary. I began stopping there to notice the "between-worlds experience" and to bring to awareness my decision to make the transition. I knew that once I entered the cathedral, I would immediately be in the land of the soul. I would meditate in the Mary Chapel, light my candle, listen to the ages-old sounds of the organ or the mass, and be easily immersed in the sacred. Then I would leave again through the between-worlds vestibule and re-enter the ordinary world. I might carry my awakened heart and mind into the village, but I would soon slip back into day-to-day reality, overtaken by the beauty of a shop window or the translator in my brain trying to make sure I knew the French word for the strength of flavor I wanted in the goat cheese I was about to purchase. The land of the soul would still be there in the background but not like it was when my body, breath and heart were paying attention in the chapel. However, having the luxury of being able to consciously move in and out of a sacred physical space that carries so much meaning for my soul's journey and my pilgrim's mind taught me to develop a strong awareness of the shifts. I could be in the cathedral surrounded by tourists who were busy locating particular stained glass windows or teenagers bored by their tour guide, but my experience, because of my mindful choice to be fully present with it, still would be an immensely satisfying return to the land of the soul, again and again.

This is the choice we present in the Dream Quest. In the

song, we open ourselves up to the intention of returning to sacred space and being changed by it. "Return Again" has a longing quality that touches memories of states of being we once enjoyed and shared. It reminds us that there is a place just waiting for us where we can remember who and what we truly are. We remember the place where we are born and reborn again. The implication is that we can mine our experiences to nudge us into the sacred. This isn't some far off state of mind that can only be attained after years of meditation or a heaven entered after a lifetime of good deeds. This is a present attainable state of consciousness available to us when we simply remember to return to it. We sing this chant many times, falling into its gentle persuasiveness, swaying and singing in harmony. I tell everyone that we will use this song to enter the labyrinth when our ritual begins.

About this time, we sing our lullaby, "Deep Peace":

> Deep Peace of the running wave to you
> Deep Peace of the flowing air to you
> Deep Peace of the quiet earth to you
> Deep Peace, Deep Peace
>
> Deep Peace of the sleeping stones to you
> Deep Peace of the wandering wing to you
> Deep Peace of the flock of stars to you
> Deep Peace, Deep Peace.

> Deep Peace of the eastern wind to you
> Deep Peace of the western wind to you
> Deep Peace of the northern wind to you
> Deep Peace, Deep Peace
>
> Pure red of the whirling flame to you
> Pure white of the silver moon to you
> Pure green of the emerald grass to you
> Deep Peace, Deep Peace

This is an old Celtic blessing, set to music by the '60s troubadour, Donovan. It is sweet and hypnotic, reminding us once again of the natural world and its loving relationship to all of us. Women who are standing begin to sway to this music and everyone lets out a relaxing sigh. One of the most important parts of the rehearsal is to let us all know that our tired bodies and questing souls will be soothed and taken care of during the Quest.

I have always had a sense that the world is animated and able to bless me. This began with my childhood love of birds. As a small child I longed to see an East Coast cardinal out of my apartment window in California. Blue birds, known as scrub jays on the West Coast because of their more brownish color, became my favorite and I even saw them from time to time. Each time I did, I felt that I was blessed. My father gave me a small plastic blue bird that fit into the palm of my hand and Tweeter became my constant companion. He accompanied me everywhere in my world, and in my imagination we roamed lush forests with babbling brooks and mossy tree trunks. There were blue flowers all around and woodland animals to play with. This was utterly unlike the dry, palm tree-studded landscape that I lived in. It was not until 1995 when I made a journey to England's Cornwall coast in May that I saw the landscape that Tweeter and I inhabited. Fields of blue bells, glades of shade trees, grottos just right for fairies and elves welcomed me when I visited Tintagel, St. Ives, and Penzance. It felt like a childhood dream had come to life or perhaps that I had stepped back into a beloved landscape from another lifetime. The quality I experienced was of all the elements bestowing a sense of deep peace and homecoming. It makes sense that the running waves and the sleeping stones and the flock of stars can fill us with deep peace. We sing this song to bring the animate natural world into the cathedral and into our consciousness.

This next song is one of mine and sets our purpose:

> Listen to the Call from the top of the mountain
> Listen to the Call from the silver wings on high
> Listen to the Call in the depths of the cathedral
> Listen to the Call and fly

Listen to the Call in the words of your teachers
Listen to the Call in the forest's lullaby
Listen to the Call in your tears of joy and sorrow
Listen to the Call and fly

And we're all called together
We're all called to love
When we listen in the stillness of our hearts

"Listen to the Call" suggests that something can happen in the Quest that attunes us to our spiritual aspirations. We are giving ourselves the opportunity to listen and even expect that we will be called out of our usual consciousness and perception of the world to a deeper or greater purpose. So often we get lost along the way of our daily lives and forget the land of the soul where we are awake to the possibility of turning toward our deeper callings. This song can help us to remember.

"Listen to the Call" came to me when I was walking in the open space behind my home in Woodacre. In the rhythm of the walk, I began to hear a drum beat, and then insistent words in my mind, nudging me into listening. At first I thought the song seemed a little bossy, but then I realized that it was a good balance to the other songs of the Quest that were quieter and sweeter. "Listen to the Call" suggests we take the initiative to find the unique and joyful service that is ours to do.

My friend Peg has had the vision of the women in the Quest being menders of the fabric of the world. She sees us as weavers, taking the strands of the world that are tattered and loose and creating a new cloth, whole and strong. By the end of the Quest when we send our blessings out into the world, I believe we all feel useful. Part of our job is to create a spiritual weaving and to give it back to the world. It is a job we can do every day in our prayers and intentions. It makes us feel useful. I have seen the gleam of recognition in the eyes of women in the circle when I make this suggestion. It touches a deep place in our hearts. Perhaps once, we women were honored as weavers of the world, our mysterious and silent work was known to be an essential occupation in society. Perhaps this recognition can occur again.

So the call can be a subtle one, not necessarily a calling to new vocation or project, but a turning to the ancient women's work of weaving body and soul, inner and outer, thinking and feeling.

Next we sing, "Come to the Circle of Wisdom":

> Come to the Circle of Wisdom,
>
> Come let your true voice be heard,
>
> Come take your place with your sisters,
>
> A circle will heal the world!
>
> We come with our stories, our lives and our struggles,
>
> We come open hearted and brave,
>
> We come in this moment of Earth's tender story,

We come to listen and save.

The circle has called us through all of the seasons,
The ancestors call us as well,
We've stood in the circle through history's turnings
Remembering to listen and tell.

The circle will hold you, our arms will embrace you
Your joys and sufferings shared.
You'll give us your wisdom, the harvest of living,
We'll celebrate knowing you're here.

Our times are calling all people of wisdom
Who love our Earth and her kin,
It's time to take our place in the circle
And let the healing begin.

This song acknowledges the circle that we are beginning to form. The circle is, of course, our inspiration and our organizing principle. It is our Way. Standing in a circle, we can see everyone equally. The song suggests what joining our circle will entail and asserts that healing occurs simply by organizing ourselves in this way. Jean Shinoda Bolen's book, *The Millionth Circle,* much like the theory of the hundredth monkey, imagines that when there are a significant number of circles in the world, something about our behavior as a species will have changed. Forming a circle is a revolutionary act! And as I say in each Quest, "This circle is forever and always. You can always come back to this place and find us. We will be here for you." The circle gives us a place to return to the imaginal realm and a way to come together that promotes equality and safety. Such a simple thing, we think, and yet when we enter the ritual of the Quest, there is a palpable "click" the moment we join hands in the circle.

The song paves the way for some of the experiences that will occur during the Quest. On a personal level, we promise that our true voices will be honored and heard. We promise to hold one another's joys and sorrows, to witness and console, celebrate and embrace. This is no one person's job. This task is collectively shared. By coming to the circle, we are putting our trust in our collective healing potential.

The "Circle of Wisdom" also suggests that the archetype of the circle is an ancient one. Perhaps our ancestors came to the circle the way we know that indigenous people the world over do. From the Indian round dance to the ancient peoples keeping warm around the fire, we naturally gather in a way where we can see each other. Over and over again I've seen how groups of diverse women instinctively know how to show up in the circle. It breaks down the anonymity that often attends gatherings of people sitting in rows.

We assume right from the beginning that we are all participants, not observers, that we are valued and that we belong.

As with "Listen to the Call," we trust that our coming to the circle is a useful act. We are called to the circle, we respond as intrinsically important parts of the whole. Participating in the circle is part of our job and in that job, we feel seen, heard, and respected. The circle is a symbol of the hope that our actions will be helpful for the good of Earth and of all beings.

Throughout the Quest, we will form inner imaginal circles and large and small circles where we hold hands. Each time when we return to the labyrinth and before we leave each other, we affirm the power of the circle again. Sometimes by the end of the Quest, the circle becomes a bit oval or fragmented. It doesn't feel quite right to anyone, and without any comment, the women begin to move themselves into a true circle. We intuitively know how this should be done, and like most spiritual practices, we have only to remember to return again to the ancient women's work of circling.

Our next songs deal with one of the most important parts of the Quest—the affirmation of the feminine face of God. For me, it has been the personal aspect of Mary or Green Tara from the Buddhist tradition that has warmed my more expansive and impersonal notions of the Divine. I remember watching a film where Carl Jung answered the question, "Do you believe in God?" by saying that he knew God. I feel the same way. God isn't some thing I believe in. I simply know God. When it comes to praying or honoring, though, an archetypal figure is a comforting part of the equation. While our adult, rational minds may scorn the White Man with a Beard or a Brown Buxom Woman, our intuitive hearts delight in beautiful representations of wise teachers and masters, and melt in the imagining of being held by the Mother of God. Our psyches are programmed to receive these kinds of images.

For many of us raised in the Judeo-Christian tradition, our images of "true" divinity have been limited by the patriarchal God the father and His only son. Even when we understand these conventions to be part of a particular tradition and the mythological realm of that tradition, they work on our psyches to exclude the feminine from our deep archetypal worship. In the spiritual pantheon, God the father ranks highest, just like Dad and the president. We seek in the Quest to bring a balance to this bone-deep experience by calling on the Divine Mother. While the sacred feminine includes many archetypes—maiden, mother, crone, the warrioress, the sage, the fiercely compassionate one—we begin with the mother archetype in order to activate early, tender memories and associations deep within the psyche.

The women who come to the Quest hail from many traditions: Christian, Jewish, Pagan, Buddhist, Indigenous, or no tradition at all. Some of us who have grown up Catholic have known Mary in our childhoods and have found comfort in her presence. The church has portrayed her as ever-faithful, obedient, and the victim of unbelievable suffering. She holds the record for sacrifice. In the Quest, we welcome Mary as one of the mothers of the world, but suggest that we might open the door to fleshing out her essence and reclaiming all aspects of her power.

Many Questers have embraced the Pagan tradition of our European ancestors' notion of the goddess and relate to her mother aspect as the Divine Mother. This encounter with the archetypal Mother is not tainted with patriarchal subjugation. For those Questers whose background is Protestant, the idea of a feminine divine presence can be foreign. Mary only shows up at Christmas in many denominations. Buddhists accustomed to Quan Yin and Tara often think of her when we call on the Divine Mother. Any Questers who have embraced the Hindu tradition have a pantheon of images of mother goddesses, from Durga and Kali to sweet Saraswati.

Whatever belief systems we bring to the circle, we have the opportunity to simply try on the experience of calling on Her. When I first heard the next chant I was deep in meditation in a yoga class. Its simplicity allowed me to come to the Mother as a child. I did not know who she was at the time, but the song was soothing to me. My relationship with my own mother had been problematic, and I rarely asked her for anything. Much of what I know about nurture and tending came from my friends, both male and female. I learned how to mother my daughter from some mysterious source that was beyond question. I always knew what to do and how to be with my daughter, much as I had with my special-education students before her. I now know that this mysterious source was, in fact, the stream of love and connection we call the Divine Mother. It is a stream that manifests throughout our troubled world and flows through compassionate and tender exchanges between human beings in every tradition.

So we call on this Divine Mother and during the following song, we remember that we are Her daughters and ask for Her help:

> Come into my life, Divine Mother,
> Come into my life, Divine Mother,
> Come into my life, Divine Mother,
> I love you.
> Hold me in your arms, Divine Mother,
> Fill me with your love, Divine Mother,
> Show me the way, Divine Mother,
> Teach me how to pray, Divine Mother.

Always, this song brings a quiet and depth to our circle. As we entertain the notion of a Divine Mother, most of us begin to open in our own ways. I look around the circle and see some eyes enraptured and other eyes in deep sorrow. Still others seem worried or aloof. A few women have shut down at this moment, sensing a worshipful devotion that reminds them of places in their lives when they have been exploited or unseen. Sometimes when a woman has been abused and not kept safe by her own mother, it is very hard to trust in any mother. All of these ways of relating to Divine Mother are fine in the circle. I ask everyone to simply be patient enough to see what will happen through the Quest and suggest that we all have complex relationships with the Mother, whether she is a divine or human, within our lives or inside our psyches.

The next song, "Mother We Sing to You," is more of a declaration about what we might bring to the relationship with the Divine Mother:

> Mother I sing to you,
>
> Mother I bring you my passion and presence.
>
> Mother I sing to you,
>
> Mother, I bring you my life,
>
> Opening to holy sight
>
> Weaving the streams of my life,
>
> Building a paradise,
>
> Healing the fear and lies,
>
> Mother, I gaze through your eyes.

This song came to me first as a tune while I was walking around the Tor, a conical hill in Glastonbury, England. Glastonbury is a mystical wonderland, home to celebrations of the great goddess and the Arthurian mysteries. By this time in my life I had begun to experience Mary as my touchstone in the realm of the sacred feminine. I felt a reverence and honor of her and found myself declaring my promise to her; that through passion and presence, I would see through her eyes, love through her heart and live through her womb.

The first verse declares that we approach her with our passion and presence. We acknowledge that our soul's bright light is a gift. We commit to open to the most far-reaching intuitive perception, and we commit to understanding and working on our lives like the weavers of a fine tapestry. We also acknowledge that we have a responsibility to create a paradise on earth. To create that paradise, we must first heal the fear and lies that exist in our lives. Doing all of these things brings us to the place where we can gaze out at the world through her eyes. When we remember, when we vow to be present, when we open to spirit, we become her eyes in the world.

I believe that the most crucial aspect of the mother archetype is that we can carry her energy through living our lives in spiritual integrity. She sees here on earth through our eyes. In contrast to the transcendent deities who look down on us from afar, the mother manifests here on Earth, through our bodies, here, now in our own human consciousness.

I hope that bringing her to our consciousness as a sacred

embodied divinity can change the way we view the world. Through participating in a relationship with her where we promise to be her eyes, heart and womb, we affirm the sacredness of the body and by extension the sacredness of the earth. When I practice gazing through her eyes, I see that some of the terrible things that happen in this world are done out of the suffering of the perpetrators. I access another level of compassion.

In the next verse, we move into another way of relating through the Mother:

> Kindling my heart to flame,
> Free from the guilt and shame,
> Breathing the beauty of life.
> Hearing the orphan's cry,
> Finding the lullaby,
> Mother I love through your heart.

The song invokes the realm of the heart—feeling, loving, being. As we seek to embody the sacred feminine, we must rely on the kind of consciousness that is qualitatively different than our rational understanding. Something changes in our perceptions when we breathe into our hearts. When the heart ignites, we let go of the anxious story of our minds and enter into another way of being, free from the guilt and shame that plague so many of us.

By breathing attentively into the heart, we open a door to the beauty of life. When we arrive at this consciousness, our empathy is awakened and we can hear the orphan's cry, whether that orphan be a homeless child shown to us by a charity on our television screen or the abandoned child that dwells in our psyche. We can find a lullaby to soothe that child when we open to the heart's unique energy through our breath. Telling the mother that we are willing to love through her heart, we can join with her energy. This way we again embody the Divine Mother energy through action on Earth.

The final verse brings us to the realm of a woman's creative center:

> Tending the new-sown seed,
> Free from the strife and greed,
> Cherishing life at its source.
> Birthing in strength so light,
> Full of a tender might,
> Mother I live through your womb

Whether giving birth to children or gestating an idea or a project, women have the ability to dwell in the physical and energetic space of the womb. I believe that all women have the potential to occupy this part of their bodies, whether or not they have a functioning uterus, whether or not they have been abused. It is part of our birthright to intuitively know about the energetic experience of gestating and birthing. We tune into this center by deep belly breathing. As we stand in the circle together, we place our hands on our bellies and wait until our breathing relaxes to the point where our hands gently move in and out. We take our time. Sometimes a lifetime of shallow breathing or the trauma of sexual abuse makes even finding the belly in our awareness a challenge. With our eyes closed, through the power of gentle persuasion, we eventually are able to enter the realm of the womb.

So many women have troubled relationships with their wombs. Perhaps they have had difficult pregnancies or deliveries. Perhaps they have been raped, their precious bodies and spirit attacked and used. Perhaps they are past their fertile years and have been told that they are "dried up." Perhaps they have had a surgery to remove a diseased reproductive system. Perhaps they buy into the cultural ethos that bellies should be flat and toned, and they judge their own belly accordingly. Perhaps their monthly menstruation has been a "curse," causing pain or disturbing psychological states. So many women are alienated from this part of their bodies that they find it difficult to relate to, let alone celebrate, the magic of this ultimately creative human organ.

I remember when my daughter turned 13. We created a coming-of-age ritual to honor her new womanhood. It was to have been in the May garden, but for the first time in her life, this day brought a rainstorm. Undaunted, the women guests, her grandmothers, aunt, and family friends went to her bedroom on the lower level of the hillside house, while the men stayed upstairs learning a song to sing to her after our ritual. Each woman had brought a small gift representing what it meant to her to be a woman. When it was my friend Anne's turn, she patted her pregnant belly and said that she felt that the greatest gift of being a woman was the ability to "shape-shift" and that she hoped my daughter would experience this ability in many ways in her life. I was so grateful to Anne for bringing this into the circle. I could feel a sense of surprise in my older relatives, even a bit of discomfort among all of us. What she had stated was so obvious and yet there has been little room in our culture for declaring the power of this most basic magic.

Fifteen years later, my daughter took me to an installation at the San Francisco Museum of Modern Art. It was a video piece on a large screen. Half of the screen was filled with images of the inside of a woman's womb up close and pulsing, a vision of blood and viscera. On the other side of the screen a young woman is walking cheerfully down a city street. She has a lovely yellow skirt on. She smiles. The camera moves to the back of her skirt and a bright red spot of blood. I instantly remember the same sort of spot appearing on my white skirt in eighth grade and the adolescent embarrassment and shame of having been caught bleeding. The camera then picks up on several men, young and old, who notice the blood. They stop. Expressions of awe come over their faces. They begin to follow the young woman. Eventually they catch up with her and bow down before her. She graciously anoints their foreheads with her blood. They gaze at her with reverence.

I mention these two examples because they are relatively rare in my experience. I wonder if paying attention to the womb in all its physical and symbolic aspects might be one of the most revolutionary things that we could do. Certainly this song, the practices of breathing into the belly, and the suggestions about gestating our dreams and visions are steps in the right direction.

The verse invites us to tend a new-sown seed. How many times do we have a vision, a thought, an awareness that gets attacked by a vigilant critical voice before it has a chance to come to fruition? If we imagine that we can plant this idea in our imaginal wombs and then tend it with the breath, it has a chance of taking hold and growing into its potential. Breathing it into the belly's nurturing interior takes away the strife and greed that attend our more negative patterns. Day by day, tending our ideas and hopes in this way leads to a birthing in our lives, an actualization of projects, dreams, and visions.

Let me give you an example. When I plant this book into my imaginal womb and tend it, just like I tended my daughter while I was pregnant, words can actually emerge effortlessly on the page when I sit down to write. When I try to force the process, judge my progress or skill, and create arbitrary agendas for its emergence, not much happens. When I read this book after a seemingly endless gestation, I notice that a life has been growing here, with a spirit of its own. I am humbled by what life has done through my womb.

Women forget that we have this sacred process etched into our biology. We can remember it in so many ways in our lives, let it enhance our more active routines, and bring a harmony to our existence.

So this song has many levels of meaning. Foremost, it is an active declaration that we are here to embody the sacred qualities of seeing eyes, loving hearts and living wombs. The Divine Mother has all of these aspects. She is here on earth, seeing, loving, gestating and birthing. She embodies life in a visceral and immanent way; so do we.

This song completes our rehearsal. We pause. Too often we forget to give the notion of sacred space its due. So we take a moment to remember that we can create a different state of consciousness, that we can enter into the land of the soul, that tonight we can expect to be carried into a feeling of empathetic connection with one another and with the world of spirit.

Chapter Five
Toward the Land of the Soul

Is the soul solid, like iron?
 Or is it tender and breakable, like
the wings of a moth in the beak of the owl?
Who has it, and who doesn't
I keep looking around me.
The face of the moose is as sad
as the face of Jesus.
The swan opens her white wings slowly.
In the fall the black bear carries leaves into the darkness
One question leads to another
Does it have a shape? Like an iceberg?
Like the eye of a hummingbird?
Does it have one lung like the snake and the scallop?
Why should I have it, and not the anteater
who loves her children?
Why should I have it and not the camel?
Come to think of it, what about the maple trees?
What about the blue iris?
What about the little stones, sitting alone in the
moonlight?
What about the roses, and lemons, and their shining
leaves
What about the grass

Mary Oliver

Five

With the rehearsal over, I explain that we will soon declare the beginning of the Quest. I invite eight of the small group leaders to stand as guardians in the four directions of the labyrinth. Two leaders stand in the South, which in the Plains Indian tradition is the direction of trust and innocence. Women can walk through this "gateway" if they feel drawn to working on their childhood experiences. Perhaps someone wants to awaken their carefree childhood self during this Quest. She will be served by this ritual reminder of entering from the South.

In the West, land of the hibernating bear, women who want to declare their desire for dreaming and introspection can enter the labyrinth through this portal. Women who are prone to dwelling only in their logical and rational minds might emphasize their desire to explore the more feeling realm of the inner world by coming into the labyrinth from the West. By the same token, those who need a thinking balance to their loud emotional lives might choose the North, direction of wisdom and a clear mind. The buffalo is the totem of the North, a creature so replete that he gives away everything to the people with his body, providing food, clothing, and shelter. In the East, women can explore their soaring visionary mode of being. Land of the eagle, the East encourages the far-seeing quality of intuition.

Some women are familiar with this schema, some are not. The choice of directions brings up the variety of ways we are able to be in the world. In the Native American Indian cosmology, we are privileged to walk around the medicine wheel of life, experiencing the gifts of vision, trust, dreaming, and wisdom. We might have a predilection toward being a dreamer or visionary but our opportunity is to be familiar with all of the ways of being. We can experience the gifts and limitations of each direction. Being a good weaver of these different modalities is a way of experiencing the art of creating an integrated life.

These directions can also correspond to the four functions of Jungian psychology: thinking in the North, intuiting in the East, sensing in the South and feeling in the West. Jung points out that wholeness comes about from embracing even the inferior functions. This is one of the reasons we always include some hands-on crafts for those of us more comfortable in the dreaming or intuitive realms. Making something with our hands engages the sensate function, much as journaling engages the mind. The songs and meditations inspire our feeling and intuiting. We want the women to have a full range of experiences.

I trust the power of evoking the four directions because of how useful I have found the practice to be in my own life. The archetypal quality of "fourness"—seasons, elements, the arms of the cross, the races—seems to be one of the ways that our psyches organize the universe. I remember a camping trip in my twenties when I was first exploring the Indian cosmology. I built medicine wheels everywhere, on my altar, at the beach, in the woods, on the table in my office. Each would have a symbol representing the quality of each of the directions. I would ask for a blessing from each direction, seeking the wholeness I craved, wanting the gifts of feeling deeply, sensing thoroughly and joyfully, seeing far and coming to a wise integration of my experiences. Each time I made a wheel, I would feel a sense of order and safety, elements missing from my chaotic childhood. Here was a way to always move from any one way of looking at a situation onto another within the context of the whole. If my feelings were too enormous, I knew that they could be resolved by a turn of the medicine wheel toward wisdom, something that would help me make sense of them. If I wandered too far out into the ethers via my soaring intuition, a turn of the wheel would return me to grounded, sensate experience. I loved this whole paradigm.

On this particular camping trip in the Trinity Alps of California, I was building a wheel on an outcropping of rock. I had found tiny pebbles to represent the minutia of the grounded South. A crystalline stone held the clarity of the North. A concave stone held some water for the West. I placed fallen branches to link the directions in a circle, but I couldn't find anything in the landscape to hold the energy of the East. I scoured the area for a feather, a bird-like shape, anything to symbolize the unbounded flight of intuition.

Discouraged, I came back to the circle and stood in the middle. It was then that I noticed that when I faced East according to my compass, that East was the direction where the outcropping dropped off, opening to a vista just begging for flight. I felt like my prayers had been answered and that for all my contrived symbolism, the world had something to say about this wheel. I experienced a strong sense of the creative relationship we have with life—if we give it a chance—magical on one level, deeply reassuring on another.

I call the women to the circle with a resounding "Let the Quest begin!" Slowly, they remove their shoes and find the portal that calls to their intuition. We begin singing "Return Again." The small group leaders standing at each portal greet each woman, one whispering "remember" into her ear and the other anointing her forehead with holy water from the Chalice Well. Women walk onto the labyrinth, relaxing into the rhythm of the song, and finding their way in the container of the labyrinth.

Preparing the Body

> It is amazing that our souls—our eternal essences, with all their hopes and dreams and visions of an eternal world are contained within these temporal bodies.
>
> Marion Woodman

After everyone has entered the portal they have chosen and begun to mill around on the labyrinth, I ask them to come to rest in a place that feels good to them. Some women have already stopped, others are dancing around, still others look for the pathway they are used to when they enter a labyrinth. I ask everyone to gently close their eyes and allow the breath to become the center of their attention. There is no need to change the depth or quality of their breathing, only to take the opportunity to observe it as it comes and goes. I ask everyone to slightly bend their knees and to sway if they get tired, but to continue to maintain a sense of stillness in their consciousness. As everyone focuses on watching their breath, I suggest that they begin to notice the out breath and consider that every exhalation is an opportunity to let go of anything that is ready to leave us, whether it be a feeling, a thought, or a sense of discomfort in the body. I suggest that we each sigh on the next out breath, hastening that letting go. Since this is a Friday night and I know that everyone has had some stress getting to the cathedral, I ask each woman to allow herself five or six good sighs to begin the releasing process that is part of entering the Quest. I remind everyone that this letting-go process can go on indefinitely, and that breathing always gives us the gift of remembering how to release a thought or feeling when we become aware of it.

Next we focus on the inhale. With each in breath, we have the opportunity to notice how we are receivers of life. Life-giving air rushes into the vessel of our bodies each time we inhale. I suggest that we experience this life force consciously, noticing that the breath may reach deeper and deeper into the body as we are doing this exercise. Welcoming the in breath, we can welcome other things we may need right along with it. We can call for healing and breathe it in, along with relaxation, peace, warmth, or harmony. These things can be breathed right into the body, into every cell. As we begin to fill with whatever we need, so too can we consciously release anything that is stuck or uncomfortable on the out breath. As we empty ourselves of unwanted or unnecessary energy, we become aware that conscious breathing is a mechanism to cleanse and purify our bodies, minds, and souls.

The next part is adapted from an exercise that I learned from movement master, Stuart Heller, which he called Touch, Accept, and Release. It involves scanning the body with our awareness and noticing if any place calls us to touch in with it in our awareness, imagine that we can breathe in and out of the place as though it had nostrils and breathe in the healing qualities that we need. We touch into the place that calls, perhaps even laying a hand on our hearts or abdomens, and breathe. Then we notice if there is a message that this place has to offer us or if there is anything that we need to say to this place. After several breaths, we concentrate on the exhale once more, releasing this place and its distress. We have touched in, accepted our experience, and then released it.

Maybe a woman comes to the circle with a tight neck. As

she breathes into that painful spot, gently placing her hand on it, she might notice that her neck needs to stretch. She may also notice that there is a situation in her life that is literally giving her a pain in the neck. Another woman may notice the tension in her jaw and, after a few mindful, accepting breaths, notice that there are words that she longs to express. Sometimes there is not an easy metaphor and the body in its wisdom simply needs to release. The meaning may come later. Centering on the sensations gives us the opportunity to bypass the mind. We may think that we know why we are suffering, but sometimes the body knows an entirely different story. If I touch in right now, here at the computer, I find my chin calling me. As I breathe directly to my chin, I find that it is jutting out and tense. Breathing into it, I find that it resents having to work on a beautiful day. "Argh," it says, "get on with this." I listen, and the breath begins to fill more of my body. I consider my commitment to this work and let my chin know that there will be time for a walk later, it begins to return to its more aligned position and I promise myself to sit in alignment even at the computer. I then can release the chin from my awareness, feeling more at ease and, this time at least, free of the resentful emotion.

When I do this exercise at the Quest, I often notice that my belly is tight—literally holding onto all of the preparations for the Quest—and that it longs to let go so that I can enter into the flow of the experience. Awareness and breath can ease that release and bring me more into the present moment. I find that the more I do the exercises along with the participants, the more I am showing them how to do them rather than telling. If I relax, I am signaling energetically that it is safe for the participants to relax as well.

After several rounds of listening to places that call to us in our body, we tune into our hearts. In the same way, we breathe into our hearts, taking time to notice the state of openness or contraction we feel. We listen to the message the heart has to share and release anything at all that is willing to be released. Often I'll use the metaphor of the heart as a rose. I ask how many of the rose's petals may be open at this moment. There is no right answer, simply an opportunity for awareness. We then breathe gently to remind the rose that it can open just a bit more when it is ready.

The Inner Circle

The Guest House

This being human is a guest house.
Every morning a new arrival.

A joy, a depression, a meanness,
some momentary awareness comes
as an unexpected visitor.

Welcome and entertain them all!

> Even if they are a crowd of sorrows,
>
> who violently sweep your house
>
> empty of its furniture,
>
> still treat each guest honorably.
>
> He may be clearing you out for some new delight.
>
> The dark thought, the shame, the malice,
>
> meet them at the door laughing,
>
> and invite them in.
>
> Be grateful for whoever comes,
>
> because each has been sent
>
> as a guide from beyond
>
> Jelaluddin Rumi,
translation by Coleman Barks

After we have attended to our bodies, it is time to create the first circle of the Quest. This one is an interior circle of the sub-personalities of each participant. I take this notion from psychosynthesis, a psychological theory that posits we each have many parts to our psyches and that knowing them, experiencing them, and ultimately having productive communication with them can lead to wholeness. Like the Rumi poem cited above, we can imagine ourselves as a guesthouse, opening to receive the parts of ourselves that need recognition and healing.

We start with the youngest part. Breathing into the heart, I ask the women to visualize themselves as young girls. I remind them to trust that our psyche will show us just the right image and age. I ask them to feel or see this young version of themselves. If they have been to other Dream Quests, I ask them to notice if this is the same girl they saw the last time or a newer version. We watch her and ask her what she has to say to us. Does she need attention or healing? Does she have a gift for us? Is there something that we need to know from her? After receiving answers to these questions, we ask the girl to join us in an inner circle centered in our hearts. We note her reaction and our own in making this commitment to her.

Most of us have heard of the inner child and perhaps have worked with this idea in our individual psychotherapy. My intention here is to invite a visual and kinesthetic experience of the inner child. One woman reported seeing a 9-year-old version of herself in this exercise—the age she was the year before her abuse began. Having this vision gave her hope for reclaiming a lost innocence. The women who come regularly to the Quest use this exercise to check in on how they are healing different wounds from different moments of their childhood. Women report that it is easier to get into this experience standing in a circle with other women instead of alone with their therapist. No one needs to share what she sees or hears unless she wants to. Knowing that we are not alone seems to help bring out the "inner girls" who need our attention.

When we finish this first inner meeting with what I begin to call our Maiden selves, we return to the flow of the breath, concentrating on the receptive inhale and the releasing exhale. We spend several moments just breathing.

Next we imagine ourselves as the Crone, inviting a face that is older and more experienced in life than we are to appear in our imaginations. We repeat the same process of questions, asking the Crone what she needs from us and if there is anything she has to tell us. We notice how we feel seeing this older version of ourselves, and then request that she join the young one in our internal inner circle. If we are willing, we breathe her into this inner circle. Sometimes it is frightening to imagine ourselves old. I always emphasize that we should check our willingness to receive these images. It is up to each individual woman to decide how she will populate this inner circle.

After the Maiden and the Crone, I ask us to imagine a good and loving Mother inside of our psyches. What would she say to us? What does she need from us? This can be a difficult imagining, but all of us do well to identify a kind and constant mother presence in our psyches. We want her installed to answer unfair criticisms and protect us from anxiety.

We continue with this exercise, inviting other aspects of

ourselves to come to consciousness. This may involve a shadow part of ourselves that we have not been comfortable looking at, but which has controlled our behavior on some level. We repeat everything we've done above, and ask this part for a message, if she needs something, and if there is a gift she bears. Once we have made contact, we again notice what our experience of this part is like and, if we are willing, we breathe her into the inner circle.

We all have many sub-personalities and each aspect of ourselves is welcome at the Quest. Here we cannot be "too much" or "not enough." Every part of us is welcome. I invite the women to discover more parts of themselves throughout the Quest and to use all the creative and healing modalities that we have assembled to express their discoveries. Maybe someone can create a doll to represent the inner girl or try on the Crone mask to get in touch with the wise woman she seeks. Women have told me that long-lost parts of themselves have appeared in these exercises—little girls who were abused or creative parts of themselves that they have not been able to express. Some women are soothed by the presence of a beautiful and wise crone who greets them and let them know that everything will be all right. Encountering a warm and accepting mother can counter the effects of a shaming, critical mother from our childhood.

Probably the most dramatic expression of this exercise came with a woman at the Portland Quest. She was a very intuitive person and had done this exercise for several years. At one Quest, when she searched for the Crone, she could not find her. She was upset by this and then several weeks after the Quest, discovered that she had a rare form of breast cancer. She lived with her cancer for several more years and eventually passed. She attended her last Quest just a month before she died, long before she was a crone. She was able to heal into her death with the help of many in the Portland Quest community. She was glad to be in touch with her intuition and to prepare for her passing with the help of her circles.

After creating this inner circle, I ask all present to allow a dedication to arise in our minds. To what will we dedicate ourselves during this particular Quest? Once we have put words to this dedication in our minds, we imagine holding it between our palms and gently kiss our fingertips to seal our promise to ourselves.

Greeting Each Other

"All real living is meeting." Martin Buber

Now it is time to shift our attention from the personal inner circle to the other women on the labyrinth. I ask the women to slowly open their eyes and to take a look around at all the women who have come together to share this experience with them. We begin a Greeting Dance adapted from the Dances of Universal Peace. I ask everyone to find a partner and begin by holding hands.

This creates the first "outer" circle. The partners gaze into each other's eyes, all the while breathing, feeling their feet on the labyrinth floor. In silence, I ask everyone to let themselves see and be seen, to let the masks that we all wear slip away. I acknowledge that this is a difficult exercise but one that generally takes us to the heart. After a few moments, we all move our hands to eye level and touch our thumbs and forefingers together to create a triangle that makes a tiny window to look through. Faces soften at this moment and sometimes reflections of the young ones that we called into the inner-circle exercise make their appearance in a game of hide and seek. We then open our arms high and wide, physically expanding our chest muscles and therefore our hearts. We then place our right hand gently on our partner's heart chakra and our left hand over their right hand. Closing our eyes, we tune into our partner's breath and feel for her heartbeat. We meet on this level, intimately and simply. After a few moments, we look into each other's eyes and then give our new friend a hug. So many times when I have done this exercise I feel the tears well up in my eyes because I see so many women have moved deeply into their feelings. I quote part of a poem written by Adela Karliner as a counterpoint to the words from the traditional Jewish prayer book, "I thank God I was born a man." Her poem states:

> For the blessings of tears,
>
> I thank God I was born a woman.

It is so tender to meet in this way. Without roles and status or having to "do" anything, we encounter another human being, in the heart.

All together, we greet five or six partners in this manner. I ask the women to look into their partners' eyes and see a mother, a sister, a daughter. I ask them to see a woman whose heart has broken open many times, just like theirs has, as well as a woman who has known immense joy. I pay attention to the qualities of these encounters as we proceed, adjusting my instructions accordingly, and I give each woman permission to experience whatever reaction she has during this exercise. Sometimes women are afraid to be seen by others and find it difficult to meet in such an intimate manner. Sometimes women see their long-lost grandmother in the eyes of their partner or are moved by the unconditional love that they perceive in their partner's touch. I congratulate us all, particularly the introverts, on our willingness to risk being vulnerable, to be seen as we really are. When we have finished this exercise, the Quest has really begun. We have tested the waters of the land of the soul and most of us have found them inviting and safe. For anyone who has been frightened or triggered by this intimacy, I ask them to continue with the process and to know that, if they feel the need to, they can talk to their small group leader or to me about any distressing experience.

Before we go on, I ask the women to close their eyes and to go back to their own inner circle for a moment, to touch into their own hearts and to let go of anything that is in the way of their being present to what is happening here and now. This begins a dance between the personal interior experience and the outer social experience. During our time together, we pay attention to that dance. So often we are "on" and have no opportunity to attune to the feelings of our interior lives. We want to practice that attunement and to notice the architecture of the bridge we must traverse to get from the inner to the outer and back again. Our inner lives are so precious, but often we abandon them in the crush of outer experience. It is important to bring awareness to the transition.

The Circles Meditation

Next, I ask the women to form two or three concentric circles around the center of the labyrinth. I suggest that we will be on this journey together until the morning and that the women in the circle will no doubt come to represent different aspects of our own stories. We can each be mirrors for the other, receiving the wisdom and healing that our sisters experience. We might also find women who represent shadow elements in our psyches and whom we might experience as triggering or annoying. For example, we may encounter someone in a small group who may talk on and on just like a difficult sister or someone who is ignorant of her denial when we have been on a decades-long recovery path. There are plenty of opportunities to judge and plenty of opportunities to let go and move on. If we become conscious of our feelings and recognize them as part of our experience, we can even have the opportunity of recognizing and finally "owning" neglected parts of ourselves. I suggest that the circle that we form will always exist and that we can each come back here in our imaginations any time to receive the support, love, and challenge that our circle generates.

After this, we imagine other circles. I ask the women to imagine their beloved ones encircling us, hand in hand; these people represent a circle of all of those who benefit by our coming into the land of the soul. And then, we imagine a circle of the deities, teachers, guides, angels and spirits who are dear to each of us. We ask them to join us in a large circle, hand in hand, embracing our beloveds, embracing us. Jesus, Buddha, Mary, animal spirits, various goddesses, and any other spiritual being that is precious and meaningful to us can appear in our imaginations, creating a grand circle around us. Next we call a circle of all the women who have stood in their own circles throughout the ages—a circle of ancestors. As we go on, I ask the women to breathe in the love coming from those circles and breathe out their own love and recognition to those who stand and have stood in the circles before. The last circle includes all beings with whom we share the planet. I call the two-leggeds, winged ones, ones with branches, ones with fins and gills. I ask that all life be brought into this circle and that we hold the whole of creation in our awareness. I ask the women to notice the connections between the circles and see the web that is woven between our beloveds and our ancestors, our guides and the creatures of the earth. Breathing in and out through the imaginal web, we can experience the interconnectedness of creation.

Now that all the circles have been called, I invite the women back into their own hearts again, reminding them of the dance between our outer and inner lives. We are in a powerful place when we can hold an awareness of the whole, all the while taking heed of our own bodily experience and needs. The notion of the concentric circles invites inclusiveness and harmony. Here we do not have dominion over the creatures but recognize our oneness with them. Here we are touched and loved by deities and spirit beings that we revere. Here it is "just us," without pretense, just as we truly are, in our hearts, living our lives.

The Circles Meditation came to me in 1988 when I was preparing to attend a conference called "Finding the True Meaning of Peace" in Costa Rica. The purpose of the conference was for representatives of all the world spiritual traditions to come together with secular leaders in ecology, economics, and politics to discuss the true meaning of peace. I had helped to organize this conference in conjunction with my friend, Abelardo, a psychologist and peace activist from Costa Rica. Abelardo is a Tibetan Buddhist and had invited the Dalai Lama to come to Costa Rica, the one nation in Central America without an Army and home to the UN's University for Peace. It was Abelardo's insight that the true conflicts in the world existed between the prosperous countries of the north and the poor countries of the south. He and the others in the worldwide group that sponsored the conference felt that there needed to be a Document of Human Responsibilities drawn up to complement the UN's 1948 Document of Human Rights. The whole conference was organized in a way that promoted the idea of what each person—and each nation's—responsibilities were. I had advanced the notion of breaking the conference down into small groups where people would spend some time in the afternoon following the plenary sessions and draw up suggestions for the final conference document. I suggested that each group organize itself as a circle, acknowledging the experiences and strengths of each member. I was thrilled that we would be creating circles to do the work of the conference.

When I had been to Costa Rica the year before, I had ventured to a place in the cloud forest where the land mass is most narrow. On a clear day, you can see both the Caribbean Sea and the Pacific Ocean. The name of this place is La Ventana, the window. As I approached this place, my intuition was on high. I laid down on the earth and felt the four directions in my bones. Like Leonardo da Vinci's "Vetruvian Man," I felt one with the world. I was exploring shamanism and Indian teachings at the time and this experience, so symbolic and Earth-oriented, was very meaningful. I had the intuition that I was supposed to keep these directions always in mind. A symbol arrived in my consciousness, a circle with an equilateral cross inside, representing the four directions. At the center, I saw two curving lines indicating dimension and spin. At each cardinal point on the rim of the circle, I saw petals for collecting the unique energy of each of the four directions. All around the circle were curving blue lines in a gesture of embrace.

Along with this symbol, I had also begun seeing interconnected concentric circles during my shamanic meditations. I saw circles and a web that connected them. This seemed to be a powerful symbol to suggest the reality of the interconnectedness of all things. I had the outline in mind of the guided meditation I would present at the conference when I left for Costa Rica. Before the conference began, I attended a sweat lodge with Costa Rican friends. This lodge had been built by a North American couple who were farming the land. The lodge itself was carpeted in lemon grass. A river flowed nearby where we could rinse off after the rounds in the hot womblike chamber. In the lodge, I shared my fledgling Circles Meditation with my friends. When we walked out toward the river, after the first round, I fainted. I said to my friend, "I think that I'm going to die now" and passed out on the ground. While I was out, I had the most intense vision of blue light all around me, and a kindly voice said, "It's going to be all right, the people have awakened enough and we are going to help you." I came back to normal consciousness quickly and told my friends the story. I realized that the blue curving lines I had seen the year before represented help from the land of the soul. I felt met by a spiritual presence. I must say that after this vision, the blue beings in the movie *Avatar* were a joy to behold!

I went into the first session of the conference the next day and presented the Circles Meditation for the six-hundred-member audience. Of all the times I have facilitated this meditation, this is one I will always remember. There had been many other introductory talks and prayers that day. When it came time for my presentation, I played my flute briefly and called on that blue presence to help my words take people to where they needed to go. People responded very positively. A young Druid from England even presented me with a rose and wanted to know how I knew so much about his tradition. My sense of the people in the room was that they had understood that all of our beloveds, guides, and teachers are present with us when we call them and that all the beings with whom we share the planet are connected with our every breath.

I realized then that this meditation, which has now been

shared in every Dream Quest, every group, in many individual therapy sessions with my clients, and with several large conferences I have attended, is one of the gifts I have been given to share in this world.

Dancing with the Theme of the Quest

Once we complete the Circles Meditation, it is time to bring our attention to the theme of this Quest. On this Halloween, we were celebrating the ancestors. We turned to the four veils made of netting hung from the balcony of the mezzanine of the cathedral, 40-feet high, above the labyrinth. The small group leaders had already pinned their photos of beloved ancestors to the higher reaches of the netting. I now called our wonderful dancer, Thais, to lead us in a dance in and out of the veils, symbolizing our relationship with the other world. Our dancing and singing actually made this connection tangible. We moved hand in hand in a long line singing:

> Ancestors calling, calling tonight,
> Ancestors calling our spirits to flight...

Diana played the harp and we moved swiftly in this waltz watching each other through the veils, letting ourselves imagine what it would be like to consciously move between the worlds.

Then Thais led us in a spiral, back on the labyrinth. We sang and danced, watching the evolving spiral we were making. At last when we were all tightly wound into the spiral, we paused, breathed, and remembered to give thanks for the ground under our feet, the blessings flowing from above, and the gift of the circle turned spiral in our hands and hearts. Eyes closed, we were again in interior space, remembering the dance between the inner and outer, collecting and remembering our experience. Breathing consciously, we danced to unwind the spiral and form two concentric circles.

Now we are ready to choose the animal cards that will designate our small groups. The cards have been individually colored by the leaders and lie face down in several baskets. Of all the practices in the Quest, this is one that we never alter. I have randomly selected the set of cards for this Quest and we ask the women to likewise randomly select the card that will determine their small group for the evening. This is the place where we give way to serendipity and synchronicity. Invariably women report that there has been an unexpected lesson or meaning in the card that they draw, even if they are disappointed that they cannot have the animal that they want or spend time in a group with a friend.

I ask everyone to breathe yet again, to come back to the simple sensation of breathing into their hearts. I ask them to remember the dedication they made earlier in the Quest and to imagine that the animal they choose will have a message for them about that dedication. These instructions are especially useful when Turkey, Possum, or Weasel are in the mix. These cards have on occasion caused skeptical grimaces or groans, and at times hurt feelings. It takes patience to wait for the multilayered meanings of these animals' medicine to be revealed. Possum, it turns out, can be a helpful teacher about the ability to stand one's ground no matter what. Turkey, symbolizing the giveaway, can provide just the right incentive to examine how we balance giving and receiving. Too many of us have learned to give ourselves away completely without understanding the need for self-care. Turkey teaches awareness of the dynamics of giving out and taking in.

A quiver of anticipation moves through the circle as the baskets are carried around, giving each woman a chance to intuitively select the card that is right for her. We sing:

> Where are you going?
> And where have you come from?
> What are you doing in this world?
> What are you drawing out of the well?
> Who will you, what will you serve?

Unlike the inviting "Return Again," this song takes us to another level. What are we drawing up from the well of our experience? Who or what do we serve? These questions are the perfect prelude to the small group where each woman has the opportunity to examine the opportunities and challenges being presented to her at this moment in her life.

We do not often have the opportunity to re-examine the countless choices that we have made in our lives, those that end up forming our identity and defining our paths. This part of the Quest brings up the reality of choosing to give over to the mystery. I find that paying attention to the story that unfolds in our lives on many levels is an essential component in creating harmony and health. What do our struggles mean? How have these patterns come up before? Is there a grander purpose to which today's challenges might relate? For example, the simple act of choosing the Elk card, an animal that invokes the necessity of stamina and reminds me of the pleasure of herding with my own gender, might give me pause to notice how keeping on task has served me and how dancing with a group of women has provided a meaningful moment on my path.

As we sing, some women carefully choose their cards with their eyes closed while others grab the nearest card. By and large this choice is meaningful. When everyone has finished, I introduce the small group leaders one by one, and then they take their women off to the altars that they have created, scattered around the cathedral floor. Sometimes there is some cawing or gobbling or a flight off to the far end of the cathedral as the women take on the animals' personae. Finally, I am alone in the center of the labyrinth. I breathe a sigh of relief and gratitude. Now, while everyone creates their new small groups, it is my job to hold the whole circle in my heart, praying for everyone's wellbeing and safety.

At such moments I often am filled with the awareness of what it has taken to launch the Quest. My friend, Anne, kindly tells me that she watches me lift the veils so that the Kairos can enter, the dream time can arrive. I feel like I have a template of love and trust that exists in my consciousness awaiting activation. My sisters, the circle, the songs, and my trust in the presence of benevolent spirits all activate that template and the Quest begins. During this small-group sharing time, I walk the labyrinth. This walk is always sweet and full. I am already feeling opened and aware after leading the initial rituals. I listen for guidance, digesting my impressions of the circle, praying for our strength and healing throughout the night. I scan my memory of the circle, remembering any faces consumed with concern or fear, noting women of strength and presence. I notice if anyone is struggling or seems lost, so that I can pay particular attention to them as the night progresses. The small group leaders know that they can refer anyone who is particularly distressed to me or other staff. We trust the safety we have created in the ritual and the skill of the small group leaders to help in compassionately holding the experiences of the participants.

During this hour, I hear murmuring and laughter, sometimes weeping, and occasional chants and animal calls. The huge vaulted cathedral absorbs these sounds of human joy and suffering and we are all the better for their expression.

Chapter Six
Intimate Circles in Kairos Time

May you allow the wild beauty
of the invisible world
to gather you,
mind you,
and embrace you in
belonging

John O'Donohue

Six

The purpose of our small groups is to give every woman an opportunity to find her voice. After the stimulation of the songs and rituals, and the fateful choosing of the animal cards, it is time to sit in a circle of seven to nine women and begin to share. Everyone's pace is different. Some women pour out their stories while others wait, digest, and decide to speak later. Still others keep silent. We aim to respect and honor each woman's way of processing.

Each small group leader has been trained in the ways of group process through her experience as a therapist or as a participant in other Quests. She is there to facilitate and share practices that help the group to come to a trusting relationship with each other. Hers is a delicate role. Her authority is clear but gentle. She encourages and listens. She is sensitive to the thread of conversation and offers practices to calm and focus the group. She might suggest a meditation or a quiet chant. For the first round of sharing, she offers a talking stick, a tradition borrowed from Indian councils, which signals the group that each woman receives the circle's entire attention when she is holding the stick. No one will interrupt her or argue with her or question her when she speaks. This may seem a simple practice, but for women who have been shouted down in classrooms or who are slow and deliberate in their process, the structure of the talking stick provides a safe practice.

Everyone has her time on the stage and the opportunity to make her voice heard. The option of passing the stick along and not speaking is always available. Even when she is silent, each woman holds her place in the circle. The leader assures everyone that anything said in the group is held in confidence. She encourages each woman to open up as much as she is willing.

One of our participants told a dramatic story of why sharing our experiences in small groups is so valuable and healing. I'll let her tell it in her own words:

> "A week before the Quest, I had been assaulted while on a routine outing to our local drugstore. Though I'd survived with no physical hurts, emotionally I was quite shaken. I was the last to share what had been going on in my life. Most of the women had talked about their work, their kids, their love life. When my turn came and I told my frightening story, there was complete silence. After about 20 seconds, one woman spoke up and said, 'Actually, I was assaulted and have never spoken about it.' And then she told her tale. After a few more seconds, a second woman spoke up and said, 'Thank you both for sharing this. I, too, was assaulted and have never been able to speak about it,' and told her story. Much to my surprise, a third woman spoke up and said, 'I too have been assaulted and have told no one outside my immediate circle.' Out of a circle of eleven women, four had been assaulted, which was very revealing. After this, our circle became an opportunity for deep sharing and—I was to learn—profound release. In the morning, two of the four women woke from dreams about chains, dark roads and lights, sunrise, and other symbolic signs that

clearly showed that the simple act of speaking openly, honestly, and in a circle of supportive, nurturing women had been a catalyst to release them from the experiences of their assaults."

Every small group has its own individual feeling and quality based on the dynamics of its members and their interactions. Each woman is unique in her need, willingness and propensity to share and the pace at which she does so. Our fundamental assumption is that everyone's personal story is important and that the wisdom gleaned from experiencing a wide variety of stories is a gift to us all. We can be mirrors for each other. Mysteriously and beautifully, as in Diana's story, women who need to hear from one another often end up in the same group.

The sharing of women's stories is crucial to the Quest. Weaving teachings from our personal life experiences is the crux of the wisdom of the feminine. Much different from a mere recitation of fact, theory or history, these are teachings that create an emotional brand of wisdom. I understand the word "transpersonal" to mean that we can reach the Divine through witnessing our lives in a conscious manner. The Divine is not something outside, beyond, or above us but rather it reveals itself in the distillation of a life consciously lived. If we reach beyond the drama of ordinary life and make meaning of its lessons, we touch the soul. Over the course of many Quests, as well as the years spent in my therapy practice, I have found that telling one's story to attentive, compassionate listeners is a first step in the process of distilling life experience into wisdom. When others empathize with that story, the interior world, often shrouded in pain, becomes part of the collective world. Being understood is a second step toward claiming the meaning that a particular life experience has to offer. When a woman can identify herself as a teacher, as one whose life experience has meaning and value for others, she begins to join the circle of wisdom.

Kairos in the Cathedral

After the small groups conclude, the cathedral becomes our playground. Diana and Portia begin to play their Celtic harps. Women leave their small groups and move to the arts and crafts room, the labyrinth, the high altar, the massage table. Some go to their sleeping bags for a long sleep. We want this part of the evening to be free flowing and open so that each woman can listen to her heart and know what will serve her at this moment. Being in Kairos invites us to listen to our desires and not simply check off a list of activities.

We set up our activities based on the premise of a good nursery school. There are enticing stations to call forth creativity, healing, and reflection. Some women are moved to spend the evening creating an elaborate doll. Some walk through the cathedral discovering the icons of Mary Magdalene and Martin Luther King or stop to light a candle near the bas relief of Mother Mary for someone they are concerned about. Everyone finds time to walk the labyrinth at least once, some taking a question or concern onto the winding path and pausing in the center to meditate. As the night unfolds before us, we experience a feeling that time is abundant and that we have as much of it as we need for soulful work.

Walking the Labyrinth

> *Solitude Ambulando*, It is solved by walking.
>
> St. Augustine

One of my favorite memories of walking the labyrinth during the Quest was when Riki, one of the small group leaders and I were in the center at the same time. This was prior to 2007, when our labyrinth was woven into a beautiful wool carpet instead of being inlaid into the stone floor of the cathedral. The rug was warm and cozy to sit on. I had entered the center and was sitting cross-legged in my favorite petal meditating. Riki is an extraordinary dancer. We have known each other for many years and she always comments on how she enjoys my mothering. She sat down and joined me in sharing the stillness that often comes in the center of the labyrinth. Slowly, she began to sway and in contact improvisation style, gently began to lean her back against mine. I responded by leaning forward, "dancing" with her touch, responding to her movement. We breathed together, swaying slightly, trusting each other's weight. In the next moment, she slid off my back and as I returned upright, she came into my arms where I rocked her, both of us experiencing a moment of mothering, sweet and strong. As she moved away, back into her own space and rhythm, I marveled at how perfectly these gestures embodied our relationship and how sweetly the Quest encouraged us to dance in this way. I stayed a while longer in the stillness while other walkers arrived in the center and then made my way back through the winding path.

Women use the labyrinth for myriad reasons. It never seems difficult to be creative about how we do the walk. We seem naturally attuned to this archetype and take to it as a way to process experiences. "Take that question on the labyrinth," I tell my clients. See what happens as you walk step by step on the meandering path. Your psyche will use the pattern, the rhythm, and the intention. It will know that you are seeking the experience of letting go, waiting for revelation, and then working to integrate that revelation. If you trust that sequence, much will be revealed.

So women walk during the night, some in a group in the earlier part of the evening, some in solitude at 3 a.m. Some walk to contemplate a burning question, some with their memory of a beloved one who has passed, some with a prayer for a new baby, a healing, or simply for the glory of God. Whatever our reason to walk, or even if we walk without a specific intention, we begin to experience the communal practice of following this sacred path. Out of the corners of our eyes, we see the other women walking, making their prayers and meditations visible through movement. We can experience contemplation all around us, in all its myriad forms. As a living mandala, the labyrinth reminds us of the possibility of dedicated, prayerful intent in the context of soulful community. It links us in a visible circle.

I remember a tall Hispanic woman in Texas who used the scarves we leave strewn around the labyrinth to heal an old wound. She had been raised Roman Catholic and participated in Nativity plays every Christmas. She was always a shepherd. Perhaps her height or ethnicity in that blue-eyed, blonde-haired part of Texas kept her from being chosen to play Mary, and she had always carried grief about this. On the day of the Quest, she took up a blue silk scarf and walked as Mary to the very heart of the labyrinth. Her eyes shone bright as she felt a new level of connection with the Mother of God.

Healings

Doris comes to sit next to me on the steps leading to the high altar. I have brought two pillows to make us comfortable on the stone floor. We sit close together beside other dyads clustered on the steps. Doris has come to ask my counsel about a difficult relationship. She is bereft and weeps quietly. I listen, hold her hands, and reflect her conflict. But what strikes her and brings her healing is the experience of being in the heart of the cathedral, in feminine space, not being ministered unto, but being received, heard, and respected.

After the first several Quests, we began to consider offering blessings at the high altar. In Grace, this altar is in the middle of the cathedral and is traditionally the province of the priests who lead the service. We are all attuned to the ages-old sacred geometry that is at the heart of the design of this cathedral, and we know that the high altar is an important place. All eyes are trained here during a traditional service. If you think of this gothic style cathedral as a human body, the altar is at the heart. The apse is the crown of the head and the labyrinth is the womb. So when we come to the altar and sit on its steps, we are truly entering a heartful place. A beautifully carved metal railing with a gate surrounds this area. Up the steps is the large marble table where the mass is celebrated. There are large candles stationed all around. We decided that we might use this awe-inspiring place as a way to invite women to have another experience of sacred space, as something personal, intimate, and approachable rather than something distant and imposing.

The first year we tried this, Sandra and I decided we would stand on the steps and offer blessings to women who chose to come up during the open time. We opened the gate and took our place and were surprised when no one seemed interested. We eventually decided to sit down on the steps instead of standing and then, miraculously, the women began to arrive. Our blessings began to turn into short conversations—mini-therapy sessions—after which we held hands and hugged. During the next Quest, I began to offer simple Reiki energy treatments on the altar steps. Soon other small group leaders joined me to offer energy work, counsel, and conversation. Women lined up to visit, often expressing wonder that we were sitting here on the steps of the high altar discussing their problems with a relationship or their sadness over infertility. Women mentioned that they were nervous to come into this imposing space, but that once they were there, they felt free to talk about their suffering and hurt. Many times I have heard a woman say that she had never told anyone what she had just revealed in the powerful space in front of the high altar.

There is a reason we designate a special place to offer healing. Life is filled with suffering: physical illness and limitations, illnesses of the mind such as depression and anxiety, the grief for the loss of someone we love, or the simple disappointment of dreams denied or deferred. When we suffer, we can leave the stream of self-love and enter into doubt and fear, judgment, and confusion. The first step toward coming back into wholeness is to notice that we are out of balance. If we can accept our hurts and wounds as grist for the mill of soul growth, and forgive ourselves, we are on the way to healing. Some suffering can be addressed in our own hearts and minds. Healing tools such as meditation, prayer, labyrinth walking, and movement can free us from the tangles of suffering and move us into the stream of wholeness. But often the compassionate witness of a trusted friend, a good therapist, an intuitive bodyworker, or a gifted spiritual counselor can make all the difference. When this work happens in community, it can be the most powerful of all. When the community of the circle witnesses our suffering we are no longer alone. Everyone among us has memories that plague us, self-judgments that haunt us in the night, fears and limitations that cause our soul's light to dim. We acknowledge all of this in our circle and offer the opportunity to share the burden, to remember the free flow of our dreams and experience the joy that comes when we are in the land of the soul. Coming to the high altar with our suffering is often a transformative healing experience.

This next story illustrates such an experience for both myself and a wonderful woman I met in Texas. At Quests in other parts of the country, without the spacious nave of Grace Cathedral, healings often take place in side chapels or small rooms where there can be some privacy. In this Quest, Carol and I were sitting on cushions in a small chapel down the hall from the sanctuary of the church. Carol is a black woman from Nigeria, but her short round body reminds me of my Swedish grandmother. Carol is intense, warm, and kind, with luminous and expressive eyes. Her English words come out with a West African cadence, and she praises Jesus for our experience. We have just met, but I have felt drawn to her spontaneity from the moment I saw her dancing the labyrinth. Her sharing comes from a heart filled with faith and her enthusiasm for ritual is contagious.

She takes my hands and holds my eyes in her gaze as she asks if I can make it so that her four sons live long lives and do not die young like their father. I breathe deeply. It is not part of my belief system to claim such special powers or make such a promise, but my heart knows that I can offer a prayer. I feel profoundly called to fulfill the healing role that I have chosen to embody this night and I say that I will pray with her for her sons.

She smiles. "In my country," she says, children are prayed for through their mother's breasts. Will you heal my breasts, the nipples, where they suckled?"

Now we are only guests here in this small room, with stained-glass windows, a pulpit, and pews. Some people already have expressed their worry that this Dream Quest might be a bit much in this Bible-belted part of the world. And I am not sure when anyone else might walk into the room. But I am given the grace to forget all of those considerations and am suddenly buoyed by an immense sense of entering into the land of the soul where what is important is trust, love, and impeccable intention.

"Yes," I say.

Carol proceeds to undo her flowered dress—so uncannily like the style of my grandmother—and removes her breasts from her bra. I place my hands hovering over her nipples and feel the warmth of her skin. These breasts have fed four sons and the energy that flows through them now keeps feeding those sons, her friends, and her family, all of us, in fact. She prays in a Nigerian dialect, fervent, melodic prayers. I breathe and pray and feel graced by the wholehearted space of truth that we have entered. I feel alive, in clear communion with Carol and with God. I pray aloud that our prayers be received by her sons and that they may live long and healthy lives. I pray that Carol be blessed and cared for. I smile at her, remove my hands, and bow to her. She smiles, buttons up, hugs me, and leaves.

There are simple, pure moments in doing healing work when everything is just right. Nothing particularly dramatic happened but I was filled with a sense of alignment with the collective heart of human being, the dwelling place of God. Here were Carol and I in Texas, opening up to an ageless and timeless ritual universe. In that place, all traditions are one.

Chanting

> Then I came up with this crazy idea just to walk out on the stage with no band at all and just start singing whatever came to mind. I actually fought the idea for a while because

> it seemed almost too radical, but it became obvious what I was supposed to be doing.
>
> Bobby McFerrin

Sometime around 11 p.m., some of the women gather just in back of the high altar and its healers. Diana quiets her harp playing, and the first tones begin to swell from Jay and her group of chanters. The acoustics are superb in this part of the cathedral where choirs in medieval times sang the mass parts in plain chant. Our voices are tentative at first, checking out how we blend and harmonize, but soon enough, melody arises and we take turns sending our voices out into the vaulted spaces. Occasionally whoops and cackles punctuate the chanting, and a playful call and response takes over. This is an activity that requires us to suspend judgment, to believe we can, in fact, improvise and create music—here on the spot—without recourse to written notes or previously agreed-upon patterns. Before the chanting, I am at the altar doing healings, but I always take a break to join this group for a while because it is so much fun. As the tones move and change, my voice finds its home and the melody moves through me. Sometimes I think about what I'm singing, sometimes I just let it flow as my evaluating mind relaxes. Soon time seems to stop and I begin to hear in my auditory imagination what I want to come through my voice a bit before it emerges. My consciousness hears the whole and rejoices in the music that trusting voices make in sacred space.

Many women have told me that this is their favorite part of the Quest. By this time, the Kairos time has settled in and we begin to imagine that we live here in the beautiful cathedral far away from our daily concerns. Of course we can make music, of course we can heal and play and dream of a new world.

Somewhere around midnight, after our yearly ritual of trying to remember how the archaic lighting system works, we dim the lights and women start to find their sleeping bags. Many of us stay awake far into the night, making art or having a quiet solitary walk on the labyrinth, but the mood definitely changes with the diminished light and it feels as though the cathedral herself is moving into slumber. Inevitably someone with a loud snore finds one of the acoustic sweet spots and we all hear the symphony that we humans make as we breathe in sleep. Many times I have awakened at 3 a.m. or 4 a.m. and experienced a sense of the cathedral itself breathing rhythmically. Gazing at the high vaults, I remember what one woman said about the nave being a giant womb and how she felt safe here, like a well-nurtured embryo. Yes, I think, we are all here, snug in our makeshift beds, questing our dreams, safe and protected in the sacred geometry of a place meant to house the pilgrims of all ages. What a privilege it is to be here in all these states of consciousness with enough time and space to notice and remember!

Chapter Seven
Morning Has Broken

The birds they sang
at the break of day
Start again
I heard them say
Don't dwell on what
has passed away
or what is yet to be.
Ah the wars they will
be fought again
The holy dove
She will be caught again
bought and sold
and bought again
the dove is never free.
Ring the bells that still can ring
Forget your perfect offering
There is a crack in everything
That's how the light gets in.

Leonard Cohen

Seven

The night is a short one and soon enough it is time for me to prepare to awaken us all. My trusty digital alarm buzzes at 5:45 a.m. It is still very dark outside in late October. I pull on some warm clothes, find my guitar, and go downstairs to the meeting hall for my cup of hot vitamin C water. Several women join me and we coax our voices into the hymn, "Morning Has Broken." Slowly, we move into the dim cathedral singing:

> Morning has broken, like the first morning
> Black bird has spoken, like the first bird
> Praise for the singing, praise for the morning
> Praise for them springing, straight from the word.
>
> Bright the rain's new fall, starlit from heaven
> Like the first dew's fall on the first grass
> Praise for the sweetness of the fresh garden
> Sprung in completeness whence His feet pass
>
> Mine is the sunlight, mine is the morning
> Born of the one light, Eden saw play
> Praise with elation, praise every morning
> God's recreation of the new day.

Women begin to stir in their beds and sleepy faces greet us with smiles. An elderly woman who joined us several years go told us she thought that we were angels awakening her to eternity. This woman came from her nursing home to the Quest because she had seen Grace Cathedral being built in her youth and relished the idea of sleeping inside a building she had long revered. She decided to sleep as near to the altar as she could and spent the night on the cushions where people kneel during the service. I remember her shining face as we passed her. Her dream had been fulfilled.

The first hour of the morning is a gentle time. We are silent with only harps playing for early labyrinth walkers and yoga stretchers. Some of us stay cozy, taking another dip into the great ocean of sleep. Slowly though, the cathedral awakens and we sense that we are on the outward portion of the Dream Quest arc. After this hour of silence, we meet in the small groups once again to share dreams and experiences from the night. Often women who haven't shared very much during the evening circle have a lot to say in the morning, fueled by art, meditative walks, and healings as well as the awesome experience of awakening in Grace.

I spend this hour in another labyrinth walk, tuning into the collective energy of the group. It is time to begin the process of taking what we have gleaned in the Quest back to the realities of our lives. I want to have the right words for this particular group to help facilitate that return. Always the practice of the labyrinth walk rewards me with ideas and insights to add to the processes I have planned for our morning circle gathering.

During one Quest in Portland, Oregon, this walk yielded a very effective idea for our closing circle. I walked the labyrinth holding a question about what to do to help a woman at the Quest who was very unhappy and expressed these feelings by complaining about everything. She did not like the kind of milk substitutes we had provided for tea. She found her sleeping place too cold and then too hot. Several women had come up to me throughout the night complaining of her crankiness. Her negative attitude had made an impact on many people. As I walked, however, I found myself remembering times when I did not feel pleased about anything in my environment and thought about how a certain whiny mood seems to afflict most women from time to time.

So when the group gathered, before we did a ritual in which we declared what we stood for, I invited the women to whine a bit. "Just be cranky," I said. "Stomp your feet and make noises." Not surprisingly, the group responded with a rousing chorus of cries, whines, and a fair amount of giggles. We had all been there before. I glanced over at the cranky woman and saw a big smile appear on her face.

After the release of this disappointed, uncomfortable energy, the women were ready to get in touch with what they stood for. One by one, they stepped forward with their declarations of purpose. One woman declared that she would leave an abusive relationship, another stood for her sisters who were survivors of sexual abuse. Yet another stood for herself as an artist, promising to get to her studio every few days. I was glad that my early-morning walk had given me the idea to state the obvious. With the release of the negative energy came the possibility of expressing the positive.

After the small groups have met for about an hour, I stand in the middle of the labyrinth and play my flute to call the women back to the circle. This is always a thrill for me, to send the flute notes high into the cathedral vaults. Like the singing improvisation from the night before, my flute finds a morning song with enough pauses to let the reverberating notes play with each other. Slowly the women emerge from the corners of the cathedral and form circles around me. I ask them to drone on two different notes and I send my flute playing on top of their voices. A pentatonic scale keeps us all in Celtic mood while the flute trills, rising and falling. When we have all arrived in the labyrinth, we breathe and sigh together.

We shake out our stiff bodies, beginning with small hand movements, then shaking our wrists, forearms, and elbows, and then gently rotating our shoulders. We shake each foot and ankle, gently flex the knees, and then roll our hips in their sockets. Next we awaken the head with neck circles and long sighs. Finally, we shake our entire bodies in a sacred Hokey Pokey. Once our bodies are warmed up, we do a variation of the Cherokee Dance of Life, bending toward the earth, drawing our hands up through the central channels of our bodies and up over our heads. Then we scoop energy from the sky and bend earthward again, tracing the midline back to the heart. Doing this movement, we breathe in whatever we need from the earth, fill ourselves abundantly with that grounded, mothering energy and then gesture with our hands above our heads, symbolically giving our grounded energy over to the sky. From the sky, we breathe in anything we need from the realm of the transcendent father, bringing that energy to the heart. After several rounds of this practice, we gesture from our now full hearts out into the world, offering our energy wherever it is needed.

At this point, we are standing in two or three concentric circles, holding hands. We imagine the circle of our beloved ones, the circle of the ancestors, the circle of spirit beings, and the circle of all the creatures with whom we share the planet. We remember the healings that have occurred throughout the night, focusing on the parts of ourselves that have been seen, heard, and respected. We celebrate that we are in a safe circle of sisters who have chosen to have this experience together. We have sung to the Divine Mother and many of us have heard her voice and felt her love. Now it is time to experiment with the possibilities of the imaginal realm, to share what we have gathered with the world.

First, we close our eyes and say aloud the names of people we love and set the intention of sending them the energy we have generated of love, healing, greater understanding, and forgiveness. We have been exploring the land of the soul and we are willing to believe that we can, in fact, share energy over time and space. Names of family, friends, pets, people alive and dead, politicians, soldiers, beings of every kind are whispered, and we sense that the circles of our lives are present in this cathedral in a very tangible way. Next, I suggest that we send this energy to places on the planet where there is war or suffering. The women suggest the Middle East, Iraq, neighborhoods of the inner city, and I think of my friend Elena in Israel who heads up an interfaith group that does daily work building bridges between Palestinians and Israelis. Having her in mind, anchors my intention in a very concrete way. Other women with friends or family in troubled spots of the world create a similar link.

What is it that we accomplish? I believe something real and powerful happens on the imaginal plane, something on the order of a radio broadcast being sent out into the world. It's as if someone in Bangladesh turned on a shortwave radio station and heard the music broadcast from here. If enough frequencies are broadcast there is a good chance that many people will be able to receive the signal that is being sent. The same thing happens with the field of energy we create during a Quest. It is a broadcast of hope and dreams, an offering of love and healing that we can return to again and again. As I always tell the participants, "This circle is forever and always and can spread its bounty out into the world. Imagine yourself standing here with us and use the circle to amplify your prayers. Remember the circle to encourage your actions on behalf of others and our planet."

When we use the power of our intuition and clear sight, we can send a powerful force out into the world. All of us have untapped abilities to perceive reality on a psychic level, to heal over the distance of time and space, and to know a layer of truth that is not available to the conscious mind. When we practice seeing with the heart in the land of the soul, another world of possibilities opens up. In that magical place we have so much to learn and to remember. I remember a Quest in Portland, Oregon, which I called Dreaming a New Way. Our meeting took place right before Barack Obama's first inauguration and we were all very thrilled about what we hoped would emerge during this new administration. There was not a dry eye as we sang:

>Obama is coming
>
>Change is his plan
>
>Peace, Hope, and Justice are near
>
>Let's hold him so gently,
>
>Pray for his heart
>
>And know that his pathway is clear

> Dreaming a new way, a new way,
>
> Dreaming a new way to see
>
> Dreaming a new way, a new way,
>
> A new way to be.

As we sang, we sent our heartfelt prayers off toward Washington, doing a bit of sacred feminine work on behalf of our nation.

Finally, the energy winds down and we all sense, like Cinderella, that the ball is coming to a close and that we have to head back into the ordinary world. We mark this awareness with Jay Newburgh's rendition of Fantuzzi's Prayer, making it the final declaration of our circle in the cathedral. Jay loves the Quest and has graced us with her beautiful voice and invincible spirit since the early days. She presents this call and response song with verve and sanctity. We sing:

> We offer you peace
>
> We offer you love
>
> We offer you friendship.
>
> We hear your need.
>
> Our wisdom comes from a higher source
>
> I salute that source within you
>
> Let us work and play together
>
> Go now in peace.

We then hold hands for the final experience of our circle. "It's not over yet," I say to the women around me and tell them the story of David, a special-needs boy I once taught. David's heart was very full, though his intellectual ability was at the lower rungs of the ladder, but one day when he came in from the playground and found me crying because a remarkable school year was about to end, he looked me straight in the eye and said with perfect clarity, "It's not over yet, Judy Tripp!" So often, we get ahead of ourselves and forget to be in the moment. David was one of my most beloved teachers.

I tell everyone that it is a Dream Quest tradition that we each give and receive at least four hugs before we leave the circle. We do that and more, then gather our belongings and go downstairs to the meeting hall for breakfast. The volunteers swoop in to make sure that all of our things are out of the cathedral for its 8 a.m. opening. All the papers and bits of cloth are removed, chairs are returned to their places, and the great gothic womb resumes her more conventional duties. I remember searching for a stray shoe the morning following one Quest, while the cathedral was being dressed up for a fancy wedding. I was crawling around under a pew as tuxedoed men prepared to welcome guests. It struck me what a magical space Grace is, able to serve a diverse range of needs, an inspiration to us all.

Grace Cathedral has a large meeting hall in the basement

crypt, and we reassemble there for a breakfast of hot oatmeal with many toppings, yogurt, fruit, juice, toast, tea, and coffee. Gresham Hall has been set up with tables for each small circle, all decorated with seasonal flowers. There is a buzz in the air as we greet each other in the daylight, giddy from lack of sleep. After breakfast, each small group plans a presentation to showcase the gifts of their totem animal. This part is great fun for the extroverts and a bit more difficult for the quieter among us. We try to avoid the obvious camp-skit nature of this performance, but some of the presentations turn wonderfully silly and bring out roars of laughter, while others are simply stunning creations of poetry and dance, conceived on the spot. I am always amazed at the clever way women come up with variations on the lessons taught by the animals. We form a large circle to watch these presentations "in the round."

I remember Johanna's experience leading a bear clan one year. She reported that her group had loved being bears and ended up sleeping quite close around her altar in the cathedral. When they presented their performance, the women crawled and lumbered sleepily into the circle and piled up together on the floor yawning, scratching, growling, and otherwise getting ready to hibernate. They then proceeded to snore loudly, which had us all in hysterics. Since it was late October, the desire to go inward and hibernate was upon us all, so this skit really resonated. Johanna told me that when she went home she prepared a huge meal and fell asleep on Saturday afternoon and did not awaken until Sunday morning.

Such was the power of the bear medicine. We so often forget the true need for simply being, resting, and sleeping; this presentation gave us a strong suggestion to do just that.

One year, the spider group stood in a circle and began to throw a large ball of yarn from hand to hand, creating a web. As each woman caught then threw her yarn, she spoke her intention for building connections in the community.

A few women have written songs or poetry during the night and these become part of the presentations along with the dolls that were made at 3 a.m. Some presentations involve the whole group in receiving the joy of hummingbird through a sing along or having their scarves and shoes burgled by the mice group seeking to bring beauty to their nests. All in all, the presentations give everyone a chance to give back to the whole circle.

When the presentations are over, the small group leaders form a circle and face outward around a table in the center of the room. The women come and stand in front of their leader, making lines like the spokes of a wheel. This puts us all in a fine position to give a shoulder rub to the woman in front of us, something very welcome after a night on the cathedral floor. One by one each woman greets her leader and receives a small gift to remind her of the Quest: a pearl of wisdom, a bell necklace to call in the spirits, a bulb to plant now for the coming spring, or a tiny mirror to remind each woman that they are a reflection of the Divine Mother. This is an opportunity for everyone to exchange gratitude, hugs, and tears. We then gather in a final ritual—a dance of universal peace—set to this Irish song:

> May the Road Rise with you
> May the wind be always at your back
> May the sun shine warm upon your face
> And the rain fall softly on your fields
> Until we meet again, May God hold you
> In the hollow of God's hand.

As we proceed around the circle in this partner dance, we greet each other again, marveling at how different it feels to meet women who are no longer strangers. After 17 hours in the Kairos, it sometimes feels as if we have known each other for all time. When I partner with someone I know, I often begin to cry, glad to give and receive this heartfelt blessing, knowing that we will do this throughout our lives and at each Quest—a reassuring moment in our year. Our first round of the dance is often met by giggles, as everyone tries to remember the words and the steps after four hours of sleep. As many times as I have done this dance, I often get the wind and sun mixed up. Everyone is forgiving, though, and after a few rounds that familiar feeling of the land of the soul returns and we all have the opportunity to meet in blessing and gratitude.

After the dance, we make one last circle. We breathe in the

blessings of grounding from the good earth, we receive the gentle blessing of the sky, and we feel the love and steadfastness of the circle through our joined hands. I remind us that not everyone we meet as we return to our daily lives has been at the Quest. I share the story that my first spiritual teacher, David Hunter, told me about how spiritual experience is a lot like growing a plant from a seed. He said that just as it would be foolish to dig up your seed to show everyone how well its roots are growing, it would be equally foolish to dig up your tender spiritual insight and expose it to the misunderstanding of a critical friend. Let those seeds grow, I advise. Keep them watered and tended, and share with those who care and understand about your garden.

Now is it time for the final benediction: "Go well, be safe, until we meet again. This circle is forever and always." We borrow an exclamation from the Indian tradition and end the circle with three resounding "Ahos", raising our joined hands high above our heads and shouting, "Aho! Aho! Aho!"

And as always we give and receive at least four hugs before we leave the circle.

Chapter Eight
The Maiden, Mother and Crone

Each woman carries within her being a map of her life. The young girl, the adult woman, and elder all live simultaneously within her soul's imagination.

Eight

Over the years, we have dedicated some of our Quests to one of the three major stages of a woman's life: her young virginal self; her mothering, partnering, adult self; or her elder, mature self. In the Pagan tradition, these stages of life are considered to be the three aspects of the goddess. The Jungians would say that they live as archetypes within our psyches. They also correspond to the spring, summer, and autumn seasons. Our mental and spiritual life is enhanced when we are able to identify the voices of these archetypes. The young one usually needs to be consulted in matters of transition; the crone voice needs to be developed as a wise witness to the ongoing process of life. Every woman needs to be familiar with the gifts as well as the limitations of her mothering side and to develop a strong, compassionate inner mother. No matter what our age, we have these three archetypes already living within us. We can consult with each one of them at any time. Over the years, we have sought to give form to these archetypes in poetry, dance, and guided meditations. By doing so, we have encouraged women to identify the unique way the Maiden, Mother, and Crone manifest in their life stories. This chapter introduces these archetypes and shares the poetry, meditations, and songs that we have used to welcome them into our midst. For a while when we were offering three quests a year in San Francisco, we welcomed the

Maiden in spring, the Mother in summer, and the Crone in autumn. During the winter, we rested.

The Maiden

The Quests that have focused on the maiden have all occurred in the spring. They provide an opportunity to meet the maiden within us as well as a time to celebrate the qualities of spring newness, innocence, virginal purity, and the adventure of the heroine's journey. In order for our culture to come into right relationship with the sacred feminine, we need to heal something about how we regard innocence and how we can help women to reclaim their virginal selves, which may have been robbed from them by sexual predators or by the demands of a sped-up, media-driven culture.

Too many women have been abused, humiliated, molested, or otherwise hurt as girls. For them, the idea of the maiden self—vulnerable, trusting and not in complete control of her destiny—is a frightening prospect. If a woman has been betrayed by family, her innocence cast aside, or her body used as a thing for someone's perverted pleasure, she has a hard time coming to terms with the joys of youth that should be her birthright. We hope to help remedy that during the Quest. By finding the innocent young girl hidden under shame, denial, and habits of mind, we can use the imaginal realms to build other experiences of trust and innocence. Like we do in every Quest, we call on the young part of ourselves during the initial meditation. Each woman has a different experience here. Sometimes she is afraid of the awkward image that appears before her eyes. Sometimes an image arrives that is younger than a trauma that she has experienced, and the woman has an opportunity to remember something light and wonderful about herself that she had forgotten. Sometimes an image of pure delight comes to mind. In the circle, I trust that whatever a woman is ready to deal with will surface and take form. The psyche is wise and quick to take advantage of opportunities for growth.

At the first on-the-road Quest in Houston, Texas, I met a woman named Sharon. Her childhood was very traumatic. She had done excellent, sustained work in her therapy before she came to the Quest, but there was something about the experience of the circle and the labyrinth that provided her with another piece of her inner puzzle. She writes:

> At the heart of the labyrinth, where one could expect illumination after the purgation of the inward journey, I knelt on one of the six symbolic petals of the stylized rose. I put my forehead to the ground, but I didn't feel worshipful. Agitated and oppressed, I could not remain long. Soon, I removed my veil and quickly journeyed back outward. Since I had achieved no insights, I could not focus on the object of the outward journey, returning to the community to share the spiritual gifts I had received. The leader of the Quest, Judith, had said she would be available in the chapel for blessings, healing, or counseling for those who needed it. So I sat

down, praying for peace and awaiting my turn. Observing her work with other women, and watching their faces relax in relief, my inner child began to clamor, I wanted some of that and aimed angry thoughts at a woman who came in after me and seated herself in front of me. Don't you dare take my turn, I thought. Finally, I sat down beside Judith and found myself weeping as I narrated a brief personal history and described the anger and depression walking the labyrinth had evoked in me. She soothed me, suggesting I walk it next time as the innocent five-year-old I once had been, and gave me a farewell hug. Feeling relief, I snuggled into my sleeping bag and fell asleep. Awakening just before dawn, I felt hopeful and ready to try the labyrinth again. As I stood at the entrance accessing my five-year-old self, I felt an impulse to skip. So I skipped my way to the center, ignoring the self-conscious internal critic who suggested that the swish of my socks on the canvas was bothering other pilgrims and that I should walk more quietly. This time as I stood in the center, I looked joyfully at the ceiling with the imagination of a child, seeing little houses and trees in the acoustical tiles. I skipped back out again, and even tried walking backwards, finishing the journey feeling young, happy, energized, and purified.

Sharon needed to give the very young maiden a chance to play and to dance and to have a carefree moment. I remember when I spoke to her that the quality of being carefree was one of the things missing in her life. Like so many women who have had to grow up quickly to tend to the psychological needs of their families, she had never had the chance to exercise the freewheeling part of just being in the land of the soul. All her life, careful and wary, she had tried very hard to do everything perfectly. The Quest gave her a moment of freedom and a moment of reclaiming her maiden self.

How We Invoke the Maiden

We sing:

> Journey on, Heroine
> Maiden of Spring
> Be protected, whole and cherished
> See your truth arising.

The maiden part of each of us needs two things. She needs healing from old wounds and patterns of behavior that have stayed in the psyche like a worn-out record. She also needs to be made new again—given a second chance at wholeness and success. These two things are addressed in the Quest.

The vulnerable maiden within is an active sub-personality for us all. She might surface with insecurity in a new relationship or be afraid of a new responsibility. Sometimes she balks, whines, or goes silent in stressful situations. We most often tune her out and soldier on, trying to ignore the fact that messages about sensitivity and unfinished business have just been activated. "Oh, come on," we say to ourselves, "I'm 38 (or 47 or 59) and should have gotten over that by now." This mocking abandonment of self parallels the kind of abandonment we might have suffered at the hands of a hurried mother or an abusive teacher. What is being triggered is the story we tell ourselves about our own inadequacy, a story that comes to mind quickly and is hard to catch because it seems so familiar and reasonable. It's easy to tell ourselves, "Of course, that's just my bad habit of taking things personally or being hurt because someone did not invite me to the party. Grow up!!!!!" Meanwhile, the young one inside cringes as we heap another measure of shame onto her wounded sense of self.

Through ritual, the Quest offers us another option. During the initial circle, instead of trying to ignore or downplay the maiden, we call her out, invite her to express herself, and focus on the nature of our relationship with her. Does she have something important to say, gifts to offer us? Is there something that we might like to give her? By doing these things, we can give ourselves permission and a language to talk about the tender places inside. Often during work with the maiden, women are able to go back to a painful incident that began the whole process of their self-abandonment, and understand when and how patterns of self-limitation or fear first developed.

For Pam, the process of identifying what she calls her "little part" began at a Quest. When I asked the circle to look for the maiden, Pam saw just a flicker of a face that immediately went back into hiding. Pam's past experience of abuse was severe, and she had compensated for her wounds by becoming a very successful professional woman who was continually busy doing for others. The Quest introduced Pam to her maiden self and gave her an idea of that relationship to the whole of her personality. Combined with therapy, the Quests that she attends regularly have given her an opportunity to coax her little part out of hiding and see what she is about. Pam's little part regularly shows up in her life these days, often with great joy. When her little part winces or retreats, Pam is quick to notice that there is a situation in her life that she needs to watch out for. She no longer overrides a voice of dissent from the little part but takes her view of things into consideration when she makes decisions about her life. With the presence of the little part, she is able to stand up for herself, face her memories of abuse, and find a deeply abiding love and respect for herself.

Much healing occurs when we allow ourselves to hear the voice of the maiden. She is often the part of ourselves with the most-ready access to knowing what makes us happy. She is often optimistic and enthusiastic. When we observe her during this exercise, we can give her a moment of attention and remember that we can consult her when making our life decisions. Encountering our maiden in a circle of other women's maidens allows us to acknowledge that we all have our hurt places and unhealed wounds, and this communal witnessing makes talking to the maiden much more acceptable to minds that are used to dealing only with "ordinary" reality. As I do with all processes of going within and exploring parts of ourselves, I add the codicil, "If you are willing." This phrase is magical because asking a maiden for permission is something that is too rarely done by caretakers. Bringing the awareness of willingness to consciousness gives us an opportunity to pause. Asking, "Am I willing?" brings our will present and engaged. I add that it is perfectly fine to be willing to be unwilling.

This exercise and the sharing in the small groups encourages women to identify parts of their stories that need healing. In the exercise, a woman might encounter a preadolescent part of herself that was more confident and joyful than her adult self is today. She might seek to explore this moment of her life in the small group and see what truncated that confidence. The healing then occurs through telling the story to kind witnesses and then creating a new story, a new perspective to take its place. The maiden part of us is often more than willing to offer suggestions if she is feeling encouraged and loved. If she finds, for example, that an insensitive teacher put her down and told her that she would never be an "A" student, she might want to imagine standing up for herself and rewriting that painful moment.

Compassion is the most important ingredient in this and every part of the Quest. It is important that the maiden is not made to feel that she is insignificant or wrong. We want everyone, all parts of ourselves, to feel seen, heard, and respected. That feeling is contagious and creates a growing network of support for the participants.

I gear the songs we sing and the stories I tell during the Maiden Quests toward young ears because we all have "young ears" still operating in our psyche. When we have entered into the land of the soul, we are open to direct healing. There is a scene in the movie *Good Will Hunting* where the young protagonist angrily decries his abusive past. Robin Williams, as the therapist, says simply, "It's not your fault." "Yeah, right," says the young man. Williams continues to repeat this phrase until at last the young man dissolves into tears as the child in him finally hears that the abuse he suffered is not his fault. By speaking directly to the Maiden, we hope to reach the suffering part of us that holds on to a shameful sense of self.

After the Maiden receives some healing, she is able to take on her role as a heroine of her own life story. She can begin to let go of being a victim of her life's circumstances. I believe we are each entitled to be heroines. If we are loved and respected in our early years, a sense of confidence and an expectation of success are installed in our psyches. If we do not receive that love and respect, we can feel insecure, inadequate, and unable to achieve our dreams. Experiences like the Quest help us to reclaim this heroic birthright and find a compass to chart the course for the rest of our lives. As the Al-Anon slogan proclaims, "It is never too late to have a happy childhood."

Here is one of the stories I always tell during the large group ritual at the beginning of the Maiden Quests. This tale emerged serendipitously as I studied the qualities of the runes we used to choose the small groups in the Maiden Quest and realized how they formed a heroine's tale. I've italicized the names of the runes to show how they became the backbone of the story. This tale has become the central teaching story for the Maiden Quests.

A Heroine's Tale

Once upon a time, a young heroine went out into the world. She felt a love so strong in her being and a light so bright in her vision that she knew that she was ready to undertake her Quest.

From some ancient place inside, she knew that it was time to discover her soul's purpose. She was ready to meet her history, her demons, and the confusing, exciting, lively, moments of her life. She set out into the wilderness of relationships, family, spiritual experience, and work.

And so she traveled far and wide, with faith that no matter how much fear or joy or even boredom she encountered, the path she trod would lead her where she needed to go. She faced many challenges of all kinds. Sometimes she felt ashamed of her fears and inadequacies and her life force became *constrained* by the heavy heart of failure. During these times she had to search out the spark of compassion, which always softened the shaming voice and allowed her to go on.

Other times, she had to learn the lesson of *boundaries* —how to discern when she ought to open herself to the spirit and energy of others and when she ought to keep her own counsel. As she learned about her boundaries, she came to cherish her time of solitude and inner contemplation and protect the land of her soul. As it was protected and celebrated, her soul flourished and spoke to her of the meaning of her Quest.

To guard her boundaries, she learned courage and perfected the way of the *warrior*. Breathing strong into her body with her arms outstretched, her fingertips alive, and her whole being infused with the fire of conviction, she remembered what her right action should be.

Other times *fear* overtook her; she was at a *standstill* and could find no solutions to the challenges she faced. Her mind told her stories of despair and spun in an unyielding pattern. At times like this, she had to learn the lesson of patience. Sometimes it seemed like she waited for insights and guidance to help her out of her inner paralysis for what seemed like an unbearably long time. At such times, she prayed for the return of hope, she sought counsel and release, and she persevered until a *breakthrough* shattered the resigned and consuming juggernaut. Again she could appreciate the moving, changing, pulsing nature of life.

Our heroine also enjoyed moments of serenity and *joy,* savoring them and storing them in her mind, heart, and body. These feelings gave her faith in the journey, eased her way, and inspired her to new rounds of learning and *growth*.

Periodically, there came times when she thought she had done enough. She neglected the practice of prayer and meditation, forgot the spiritual promises she had made to herself and others, and denied the reality of the land of the soul. She simply forgot, as human beings are prone to do. Time passed in this state, but then something inside would awaken once again. What called her back? What grace? What serendipity? Once she awakened, she couldn't believe that she had left the Quest and felt extremely guilty that she had forgotten her path and her promises. Her guilt *signaled* the emptiness she felt in her soul, how much she missed the Quest and the sorrow she felt in abandoning herself, for once a heroine, always a heroine. Forgiveness was her salvation. And as she has promised, the Mother took her back and the life of her spirit resumed without missing a beat. And so she learned a large measure of humility and gratitude.

And then there were moments along the way when she came to *gateways*. At such times, she would pause a moment and decide when and if she wanted to go on. She would take stock of all she had learned, breathe deeply and choose with a wisdom born of awareness. "Yes," she thought, "I've been around. I know the suffering and I know the joy. I have learned that change is the true constant and that I can weave the challenges and gifts of my life into the cloak my soul wears. I am the heroine of my tale."

One of the challenges of patriarchal organization is that

women seldom have a cultural support for being "heroines." Men are the heroes of our mythologies. There are proscribed patterns of attaining goals, slaying dragons, and so on, and usually it's men who are the dragon slayers. However, I think it is a positive change that mythological heroines have become mainstream in the past two generations. Starting with Princess Leia of *Star Wars,* Buffy the Vampire Slayer, Neytiri in James Cameron's *Avatar*, and a whole bevy of female martial artists, it has become more common to see women in very strong and self-sufficient roles. The whole notion of what constitutes a heroine is changing in our culture and I encourage the women to find the ways they might be heroines in their own right.

Sally is a true heroine in my estimation. Child of an abusive alcoholic mother who nearly strangled her, she is the only member of her family to escape a life of alcoholism. Sally trained first as an RN and then as a lawyer. Her last career was as a university professor. Until she participated in the Quest, she would never have called herself "heroine." She would have labeled herself a survivor, perhaps, but she would never have assumed the proactive, willful moniker of "heroine." The shift that she went through to claim this rightful title and the self-esteem that goes with it is significant. She had been very involved with therapy and spiritual pursuits all throughout her life, but the truncated wounded girl who lived inside of her denied her ability to claim herself as the exemplary woman she is.

Through the Quest, and the work she did in therapy, Sally has embraced the wounded maiden, had dialogues with her, taken her for ice cream and even imagined carrying her on her back through the streets, giving herself the experience of simultaneously being the loving adult and the beloved child. I think we all long for this inner harmony—finding love and acceptance of the child who dwells with each of us.

The Maiden Quests remind us to use the spring-time energies when the whole world renews itself to renew our souls and take up the Heroine's Journey.

The Mother

There have only been a few Quests dedicated solely to the Mother, but in every Quest the mothering aspect of our psyches is omnipresent. As we open to the Mother, the most tender, confusing, and important aspects of being a woman are brought forth. In the Quest there are four aspects to our consideration of the Mother. There is the inner mother who can be developed imaginally. There is the action of mothering others, projects, children. There is the experience of receiving mothering from others. And there is the relationship we have with the Divine Mother however we conceive of her. Ultimately the Divine Mother can inspire us as we mother ourselves and others. We can see her in ourselves and receive her though the love of others. The songs and exercises of the Quest draw our attention to these different aspects. The relationships that grow between us during the Quest are the manifestation of the potential of mothering we all share in all of these aspects.

    I would imagine that most of us welcome a nurturing, constant mother in our psyches. The attachment to our biological mothers is the primary building block of our psychological wellbeing. How we relate to our own mothers shapes much of how we relate to others in the world. If we have had a difficult relationship with our mother fraught with insecure attachment or abuse, it is difficult to trust the world, other people or ourselves. Even secure relationships have elements of disappointment, fear of loss, and periods of unhappiness. It helps to cultivate a trustworthy inner mother who becomes a voice advocating self-care and self-love. My own inner mother routinely reminds me to balance periods of activity with times of contemplation and comforts me when I am hurt. She counters the more critical voices in my psyche with compassion. And very importantly, she helps me to give birth to my work.

    In the last Quest I presented in Charlottesville, I made a special effort to connect with my own inner mother during the initial exercise in the circle. After we had brought forth the maiden and the crone, I became aware of the presence of my hard-won inner mother. I heard myself emphasizing that the women visualize the most loving, accepting and nurturing mother that they could. "See her loving face," I said. "Let her gaze at you with compassion and acceptance. Sense her constant presence."

Many women came to me afterward and thanked me for bringing that image so clearly to them. Some said that it was the first time that they had heard a kind encouraging voice in their internal dialogue

I can trace the strength of my attachment with this inner mother to the experiences I have had with the Divine Mother and to the men and women who have mothered me over the years. I can also trace the strength of this inner mother to the way I mother my daughter, my friends, and my clients. My time in Chartres with its daily meditation with Mary, my prayer practice, and my practice of giving and receiving mothering have installed a constant mother in my psyche who was only tentatively there during my earlier development. During the Quest and in my individual sessions with women, I counsel them to hear this inner mother's voice as a way of experiencing being loved unconditionally.

All of us can be mothers of the world whether or not we have children. We can practice a receptive, empathetic way of being that provides refuge for others. I remind women that our biology ensures a natural nurturing that can strengthen us to give encouragement to our friends, partners, and family. If we have children, we can tap into this way of being to help us guide and nurture our babies. For women who do not have children, knowing that we can be mothers of the world can be healing. I have spoken to too many women who feel that they are somehow lacking because they do not have children. Expanding the notion of mothering to the nurture of other people, creative projects, and the

Earth herself opens up a channel of useful energy and self-esteem.

Receiving mothering can be the most difficult of all the aspects of the mother. In many ways in the Quest, from the greeting exercise where we gaze into the eyes of another woman, to the healings that occur at the high altar, to the many informal interactions between participants, we have the opportunity to receive nurturing.

I remember Sophie who sat before me at the altar, her spine stiff and breath barely entering her chest, claiming that she was self-sufficient and strong. When I asked if I could give her some Reiki, she agreed. I placed my hand on her heart, she melted into tears, allowing herself to receive. Her breath deepened, and she began to realize that she could be strong as well as receptive.

At the end of every Quest, when the women receive a gift from their small group leader, there are two beautiful examples of women giving and receiving mothering. One is when each woman comes to embrace her small group leader as the leader hands her a gift. This gesture looks so tender and is often accompanied by tears. The other is the gentle shoulder massage that happens among the women as their small group lines up to greet their leader.

Many times, mothers and daughters have come to the Quest together. I love it when my daughter comes and when I see the daughters of my friends find their way to the circle. In 2011, a young woman came to tell me that she had just conceived after a long period of trying. During the previous Quest, she and I had a session about her fertility and she had spoken with her small group about it. This year, she again brought her mother and their great joy spread to us all. At the closing circle, we put her in the center and prayed for a graceful pregnancy and a blessed birth.

When we speak of the Divine Mother, we often do so in relation to the Divine Father. We speak of Mother-Father God and emphasize the partnership that many of us believe is at the core of the changing face of spirituality in our time. I hope that we are moving from a paradigm of domination or "power over" to a way of being that includes partnership in personal relationships, in leadership, and in our notions of the divine. Throughout history, as Riane Eilser postulates in her book *The Chalice and the Blade*, times when the feminine is honored usher in epochs of a partnering paradigm. I wrote this fable to express this idea:

> Once, when our kind was new upon the Earth, we watched how things worked. We saw that the seeds planted in the dark fertile soil slept for a while and soon enough were born into plants that grew grasses and corn and the tall, tall trees. We watched as the seasons changed and eventually the plants fell back into the earth, died and disappeared into her darkness. We watched too how women's bellies swelled when they were implanted with the seeds of life and how they opened and gave birth to new beings. We also saw how these bodies in their wisdom, when their birthing years were done stopped flowing with fertile blood, and instead held the life-creating forces inside. We watched these things and we knew deep in our bones that the great feminine principle that we called the goddess was the

source of our life force and our abundance. We were grateful to her and thanked her in many ways. We called her many names, and as our life on the planet grew more varied and complex, and as new and different ways of being human emerged in our consciousness, we told stories about our goddess that reflected the knowledge we acquired in love, in combat, in creation, and in deep solitude.

Some time ago, the stories we told about ourselves and our planet became absorbed into the great masculine principle and the goddess was no longer worshiped openly, and often shunned and demeaned. During these times we explored stories about heroism, aspiration, and transcendence. We tracked the need for sacrifice and the experience of pure mind. Always though, the goddess survived deep in us and deep in all the stories we humans told about life and each other.

Now things are changing. This womblike cathedral welcomes us, drawing us in to quest for our women's dreams and the time has come to bring the Divine Mother into this space and to call her names out loud. We live in a time when the truth of the mystery can be spoken and honored. Out of the vast void comes all things—out of the womb comes our lives. We remember the ancient ways our kind spoke of the Divine. As we welcome and fully acknowledge the feminine principle, so too can we welcome the masculine, the Divine Father, into our lives in a new way now that Divine Mother is once again honored.

At this quest, Anne wrote the names of over one hundred

mother goddesses on a long red ribbon. We read them, "Inanna, Demeter, Isis, Astarte, Saraswati, Mary, Shechinah...." and after every seven names, we chanted, "Be with us." It was very moving to say these names from the long history of our species, from every culture on the planet. We imagined these goddesses standing in circles around us, filling the space of the cathedral, bringing the sacred feminine presence into a space that was historically filled with the sacred masculine. These are the ways that we can create a symbolic balance between the Divine Feminine and the Divine Masculine.

At another Quest, we set an intention to discover our relationship with the Divine Mother and to ask her for her assistance. We made the following prayer:

> Divine Mother, We ask you to be with us, love us nurture and challenge us. Mother who is Earth, Mother who is Source, Mother of all things, we receive you deeply into the secret recesses of our souls and pray for what we seek, what we need, and what we desire. We acknowledge you and call upon you to be present to this place, to be in partnership with the Father in a loving embrace, embracing us, your children.

> We remember you in all the names we have called you throughout all time in all circumstances. We let go of the constraining beliefs and traumas that keep us away from your unconditional love, and we walk with you tonight in openness to that unconditional love.

I think one of our most moving Quests was one entitled Dreaming the Daughters of the Divine Mother. We aimed to acknowledge the delicate psychological relationship of mother-daughter within the context of the divine. In this Quest in Grace Cathedral, we set up a large altar near the labyrinth with statues of Mary, Quan Yin, Green Tara, Gaia, and the Great Goddess. We spread tiny mirrors all over the altar to reflect the Divine Mother living within each of us. After our usual initial exercises on the labyrinth, we walked in procession to the high altar where we made our prayers for healing in our personal relationships. We then turned back toward the womb-like labyrinth with its altar of mothers. One of our small group leaders whose own mother was mentally ill, led us chanting, "Mother, we call you, Mother, hear our plea, Receive us, Mother of all beings!" As we slowly approached the labyrinth our voices full of longing for whatever we had missed in our own mothering relationships, we let our grief guide us to the Divine Mother who can fill us with her loving gaze, her pure heart, her holy womb.

The Crone

In the fall of the year when the light begins to shift toward the darkening season, we honor the crone. We think of the crone as the archetypal wise woman, a woman who has lived her life, experienced the stages of maiden and mother, and has moved to another level of knowing and awareness. For most of us, the crone is an archetype that has yet to enter our daily lives, but each of us has access within our imaginations of an older and wiser part that sometimes visits our musings and dreams.

The crone no longer menstruates. The American Indians say that her blood has turned to stars in her heart and mind. The Chinese say that the energy that once descended to prepare to make life, rises upward and fills the soul with wisdom. While the attitude of the crone can visit a woman at any age, there is something important about the moment when a woman accepts herself as the crone. I remember when Alyssa, a small-group leader, accepted herself as the crone. In her early seventies, she was just becoming comfortable with her retirement. We held a ritual whereby she was presented with our Crone mask. She reported that donning the mask and then dancing as the Crone brought her to peace with her years and the responsibility of being the wise woman.

During the Crone Quests we focus on her qualities of wisdom, fierce compassion, and no-nonsense panache. For the past 13 years we have used the aforementioned Crone mask, a bit bigger than life. This visual object has had a strong effect on the participants. At first sight the mask is fearsome with its flowing grey hair festooned with lichen and twigs. Her eyes are blue and peer out of her very wrinkled skin. As you gaze at her, however, she softens and looks imploringly at you. She has such charisma that it's easy to imagine that she might very well be able to handle almost anything we might say or do. Imagine your own grandmother, not burdened by the rigidities of aging, but blessed by an awareness born of years of love and insight. We provide a full-length mirror so that each woman can try on the Crone mask and have a look at herself as the archetype. At first, everyone's fears and prejudices about aging arise. Our acculturated selves don't want to look fearsome and wrinkled because youth is so prized in our culture and age is so feared. How then do we honor this stage of being and the wisdom that it can hold? Making the identification between ourselves and the Crone in the imaginal world is the first step.

I remember my first experience putting on the mask and looking into the mirror. As I stared at myself through those piercing eyes, I began to feel a kind of power that I hadn't experienced before. It was not necessary to be beautiful or to smile nicely. I was simply present, the record of my well-earned wisdom on my face. As I spoke, I was able to find a crone's voice and a perspective that seemed blunter, more to the point than my usual way of speaking and seeing the world. I felt that I was being given permission to access things that I knew but had been afraid to express. My friend Jenny was with me when I first donned the mask. She asked me some questions about her life, and I found myself answering her very directly with authority and compassion. I saw her facial expression as she received my words and knew that she had heard my response as a message from an archetype, not merely as her friend's opinion. We had both entered into the imaginal realm.

Coming to terms with aging is a lifelong process. Some of us long for our later years when we usually become stronger in our definition of self, but most of us fear illness, diminished physical capacity, and the loss of status afforded to younger women. Being able to "try on" the mask helps us to envision the kind of old woman we want to be.

When I was in my late thirties, I had an experience during a workshop that helped me with the crone. I was leading a meditation to access the various stages of life, which is similar to one of the practices that we use in the Quest, when suddenly my face at around age 75 appeared before my eyes. Even though I was directing the meditation, I found myself quite unexpectedly experiencing the very thing that I was evoking. I literally saw my own face, very loving with many smiling wrinkles around my eyes from which a wise kindness emanated. My curly hair was grey and pulled back from my face. I have never forgotten this vision. When I think about this future self, she soothes me and gives me hope that I might age with wisdom and grace.

Women generally report being more comfortable with the prospect of aging after having the experience of the mask. They also warm to the idea that they can become wise women. There is power in this kind of imagining because far too many women remain only girls for their entire lives, afraid to accept and utilize the lessons they have learned and the authority that would come from their speaking their minds. Relating to the crone creates the possibility of claiming their power.

We imagine the crone being fierce when need be, standing by the truths she knows, being able to say "No," to affirm her boundaries, and to champion the poor or downtrodden. She doesn't have to put up with any more nonsense in her life. People honor her with deference and obey her when she tells them to stop being foolish. Our crone has had a lifetime of meditation. She knows how to access her land of the soul and she isn't afraid to make waves. The following are some of the invocations to the Crone that I have spoken over the years in the Quests that occur in the autumn dedicated to her:

> Tonight we turn our wise crone selves to the task of cultivating the tender folds of our psychic wombs. We remember the healing that comes from the crone voice within us; a voice that tells us to remember to breathe, to experience our feelings and to brew a tea of the depth and complexity that is our inner resource and supreme gift to the world.

> We have always gathered in the places of the circle to be with the darkening season. Together we embrace the depth of the inner life, its challenges, and its gifts. And together we encounter the darkness of the world, acknowledge the suffering, and search for redemption.

We celebrate the season, the shortened days, the deep cozy nights, the quieting of the sun's bright glare. We remember. We dream long. We harvest pearls of wisdom.

> Dark Crone, Grandmother of time,
>
> Your womb has birthed the world
>
> You know from every crevice of your being
>
> The meaning of the dark.
>
> Remind us to look into our caves and
>
> To dwell there not in sorrow or shame
>
> but with patient, accepting love.
>
> We are mothers of the world,
>
> Our breasts overflow
>
> with nurturing human kindness.
>
> Our tongues are ready to speak the truth
>
> Our arms are outstretched
>
> to embrace the world
>
> and to set the boundary that says:
>
> Enough is Enough,
>
> Remind us this night of October harvest
>
> Remind us of the wealth
>
> of the slow, dark season.

For this Quest, Thais created a womblike basket made of branches and seaweed. We placed pearls inside of it and then handed them out during the initial ritual, asking each woman to hold one and imbue it with her wisdom. Then we collected them back into the "crone's womb" and let them sit on our altar throughout the quest. In the morning each woman received a pearl of wisdom to take home with her. In this simple exchange of a small object that another woman had held and filled with her wisdom, we valued the wisdom that resides in each of our hearts and shared it. I still have that pearl and remember the joyful sharing that occurred during that Quest.

At another Crone-inspired quest we made this invocation:

> We call now the ancient one, who we all are, who we will become. We cloak her in the robes of youth, purity and innocence. We honor the birthing she has done. We give her the gifts of the Earth she so deeply knows, immersed as she has been in Gaia's seasons and elements, her creatures and flowers. She is with us now, born of our respect and nurture. Born of the support of ancient Mother Earth, she rises to dance with passion, with knowledge, with a no-nonsense presence. We welcome you, Crone, Grandmother face of the great goddess, manifestation of the high wisdom of the eternal spirit. Through you, we travel to the Great Mystery of God. You are big enough and safe enough to let us rest on your bosom.

Part of the beauty of the reemergence of the sacred feminine in our culture is a reclaiming of the value and wisdom of women in their elder years. Women of my generation are used to acknowledging their power, fighting for equality, and being heard to a far greater extent than our mothers ever were. Our expectations of respect and influence as we age are creating a new generation of grandmothers who want to explore their wisdom and power. We envision a world where our wisdom will be tapped and utilized. The Quest allows us to imagine how our wisdom might be translated into action in the world.

Chapter Nine
Tales from Near and Far

I will go with my sisters a 'dancing,
On the path of the Labyrinth]
I will sing and I'll dance and I'll dream there
In a place where my heart can rest

And I'll dream of a world with more kindness
Where all beings are free and whole.
And I'll go with my sisters a' dancing
On a path where our souls are home.

Nine

Each Quest has a life of its own. Clustered around the songs, exercises and practices that we always do, are themes that relate to the season, the place, the current politics, and the cultural climate of a given time. We had "Dreaming A New Way" in 2008. In 2012, we will have "Dreaming Transformation." There is a dynamic relationship between what has become "tradition" and the need to be responsive to the moment. Following are the stories of specific Quests:

The First Quest

The very first Quest was held in early January 1987. The Rev. Dr. Lauren Artress and the Rev. Elaine Gilmore had contacted a group of women in the community to create an overnight event for Grace Cathedral. There are many aspects of this first Quest that I have continued to use over the years. I was 38 at the time and asked to be a small group leader. I was thrilled to be among the women I considered my older sisters. As I scurried around finding sacred objects and just the right thing to wear, I truly felt as if a dream had come true. This particular Quest was quite an extravaganza. There were many leaders with conflicting opinions about how to create the event. The atmosphere felt chaotic and giddy when I arrived at the cathedral. I boldly asked if we could make a circle and hold silence for a few moments, something I did for my own sanity. In that silence, I realized that my destiny was somehow related to this event and that the energy needed to create it had to come from inner peace and calm. I felt the immensity of what we were undertaking. Here we were, a group of women recruited from outside the church, taking over the space for the night. We had created beauty, utilizing the twenty or so undecorated Christmas trees left over from the holiday season. They formed a grove near the baptismal font. One of the leaders had brought oriental carpets from her home for us to sit on. This was five years before the labyrinth would be our centerpiece. There were fifteen small group leaders that year, and we had outdone ourselves building beautiful altars with statues, candles, and flowers around the cathedral floor.

It was cold and dark in the cathedral. The buzz of activity gradually quieted as the time approached for the building to close to the public and open to the dreamers. When 6 p.m. arrived, there was one drunken man left in the pews. It was as if he had been drawn to what we were creating as a moth to a flame, a wounded male to the nurturing feminine presence. Someone asked him to leave. He refused. The cathedral watchman was called and insisted he move. The man yelled and cursed and stayed put. When the watchman grabbed him, the man struck a blow and there was a lot of yelling and posturing in the midst of our beautiful space. At last, one of the women who had a good deal of experience working with alcoholics sat down next to our moth and gently persuaded him to leave. The small group leaders stood in awe. What had we created here? Why had he appeared at just that moment? What was he drawn to? Did he actually experience the energy that we were creating in our ritual? Did he need us? That man, down and out, drunk, clearly wounded, played a deep role in the archetypal drama that unfolded in that particular Dream Quest, and which continues to unfold to this day. I believe he was the energetic nudge that brought the dream that has informed my life ever since and brought a deep lesson about the meaning and mission of the Quest.

After the incident with the man, the event went on smoothly and beautifully. Our small group was dear and deep. I had chosen a place beside the small baptismal font at the front of a small chapel at the rear of the cathedral. This place felt nurturing and feminine to me. I had set my cloth, candles and flowers, my crystals, rocks and prayer beads in a pleasing array. I was comfortable with my place, when I looked up and saw that this quiet spot was overseen by the cathedral's only Jesus-on-the-cross crucifix. I'm not sure how I missed Him, but at that time in my life, I probably would not have chosen to sleep underneath Him. However in a situation like this there are no coincidences and I took my unconscious choice as something meaningful to my path.

All my life, this suffering Jesus had troubled me. I did not go to church as a child although my Catholic mother would sneak me into church against my father's wishes and let me drink in the dark, pungent, forbidden fruits of St. Mary's and St. Joseph's and St. Patrick's, the other two Catholic churches in our area. I longed to have rosary beads and to be allowed to take in the body and blood of Jesus during Communion and to stay in the cool darkness of St. Mary's on Good Friday like my cousin did. At age 8 or so, I bought a rosary at Woolworth's and secretly passed it to my cousin to have it blessed by the priest. I have since come to a deeper appreciation of Christ, but in 1987, I regarded him as a symbol of the wounded man at the heart of the patriarchy. I slept fitfully on and off that night and early in the morning, I had this dream:

> I am sitting in my therapy office with my partners. We had undertaken to do some pro-Bono work and a young man from the street had come in to have therapy. We had all worked with him and believed that we were helping him. We felt quite self-congratulatory as he sat in the office, thanking us. At the end of the session, he invited me to go with him back to where he hung out. In the next scene, we are in the Tenderloin, a neighborhood that is bleak, frightening, chaotic, and gray. The young man, who had seemed so well and happy just a short time ago, turned nasty and cynical, saying, "How did you think you could help me? Are you crazy? Don't you see what life is like here?" He grabbed me and pointed me at a vendor selling some sort of meat. "See," he said, "They sell baby meat here." He laughed a hideous, blood-chilling laugh. As I looked toward the meat, he grabbed me again and said, "Of course, it isn't baby meat. This is how we get it." He gestured up to a porch where a dog was being torn limb from limb—tortured for its

meat. I half awakened and silently screamed, "NOOOOO!" with an emotional intensity I had never experienced before.

At just that moment, two women with candles and a guitar came strolling through the cathedral singing, "Morning Has Broken." There I was, the image of the dream still very clear. For a moment, as I lay there drenched in sweat, hearing the women singing the most hopeful and life-affirming song, I existed in two worlds, holding an absolutely clear and present awareness of both realities. In the same instant, I experienced the unspeakable horror of the world, filled with cruelty, suffering, and woundedness, and the expansive and graceful beauty of this world, hopeful, affirming, and healing. I will never forget that experience. Yes, this is what exists: the dark and light, the woundedness and the healing, the "No!" and the "Yes!", the crucifixion and the resurrection. This ability to witness both the joy and the suffering of this world simultaneously has become the guiding principle in my life. I believe that our hearts need to grow large and flexible enough to hold the reality of a world that is simultaneously on the brink of disaster and full of hopeful signs of change. We need to be comfortable in our capacity to hold these poles, never shrinking from our responsibility to witness what needs to change or our responsibility to harvest the seeds of hope springing up all around us. The dream has reverberated in my life both from this archetypal level of meaning and the message it gives me about my own relationship to the wounded man.

I believe that there was a reason that I slept beneath the crucifix and that reason has only become clear to me over the years. As I said, at the time, I saw the crucifix as a reminder of the wounded male that seems to be a result of the patriarchy. By denigrating the feminine for centuries, both women and men were nailed to a cross. But under that suffering Jesus, my psyche created a redemption dream that led me to value the words of faithful women singing to welcome the dawn, all the while being cognizant of the immense suffering in the world. Since then all of my work in the Quest has been to support those singing women so that through beauty and fidelity to the land of the soul, we might counter the suffering. What I have come to know as I have studied Christianity over these years is that the truest message of Jesus is utterly the same as the humble meeting with suffering and the profound belief in redemption. I hope that the Quest with its tender acceptance of the vulnerability we all share is helpful in healing the strident wounds of our world.

The Quests after 9/11

The first Quest after the devastating attack on the World Trade Center was held in Germantown, near Memphis, Tennessee, on September 28. My hosts told me that I did not need to come since there was widespread fear about flying during those traumatic days, but I decided to go anyway. I entered the airport with anxiety, and I wasn't alone in my feelings. Everyone was aware of the airline employees who had died. The flight attendants wore black ribbon pins commemorating their comrades. I remember the pilot giving a speech over the intercom, thanking us for being brave and reminding us that if anyone tried anything that we were all empowered to stop them. It was clear to me how everyone was still traumatized.

The Quests in Memphis had been true and clear. The priest and labyrinth facilitator who brought me in for six good years had a clear vision of bringing alternative ways of worship to her conservative parish. Over the years I had made good friends among the women in the congregation who looked for something a bit radical in their theology.

The small group who attended this quest sat together in a circle before we began the ritual on the newly installed outdoor labyrinth. Late September in Memphis is balmy. Chirping insects were everywhere in the lovely garden that surrounded the labyrinth. We could walk around barefoot and set up our sleeping bags outdoors. We met indoors to start. The first thing I said was how deeply I realized that we were nowhere near healed from what had just happened in our country. There were audible sighs and everyone relaxed as people do when what is obvious is named. We talked a bit about what it is like to do ritual during such a time of personal and collective trauma. We talked about the need to hear the Mother's Voice and to be prepared to be involved in our nation's troubles. We spoke also about the need to heal the personal traumas that we had encountered during our first true experience of homeland vulnerability on the world's political stage. As I always did in those days, I asked if anyone had lost a friend or relative. One woman had lost a relative and her grief brought us all to the personal level of the tragedy.

Because we were a group of small group of thirty, it was possible to introduce ourselves individually. We honored our maternal lineage: I am Judith, daughter of Miriam, daughter of Rose, daughter of Kathleen. The names of southern women filled the room: Susan, daughter of Belle, daughter of Mabel, and so on. The women began to relax, anchored by the memory of their ancestors, more able to cope with the present by remembering the lineage and strength of the past. The rest of the Quest went well, marked by prayers for the people who had been lost and prayers for the future of us all.

A month later, I facilitated the 2001 Autumn Quest in San Francisco, which always occurs at the end of October. I had chosen the theme during the previous spring: Dreaming the Crone's Harvest. I wrote this as an introduction for our program:

> We come together this evening, poised on the threshold of the darkening season, a moment when the veils are thin and the land of the soul is particularly accessible.

We come together at a moment of high uncertainty in our world, newly healing from the attacks on our country and reeling from all the violence, real and rhetorical, and the clash of feelings that accompany the violence.

We come together in this Quest for community, for comfort, for healing. We will call on four Mothers of the world traditions tonight: Mary, of the Christian and Islamic streams; Tara, of the Buddhist stream; Kali, of the Hindu stream; and the Shechinah, of the mystical Jewish stream. We will ask that they stand for the voice of the Mother in all traditions gifting us with the inspiration of devotion to God, compassionate understanding, fierce presence, and the ability to dwell in the heart of the divine.

Please receive the inspiration we will offer to delve even deeper into your own heart and hear the Mother Voice. Work to let go of anything that is in the way of your own expression. The world needs to hear from women, from Afghanistan to Washington, D.C. It is time speak and sing and dwell with the truths that we have harvested from our lives.

Be welcome here in our great gothic womb, among sisters. Explore what feels appropriate to you; sleep when you need to, ask for help when you need it and be blessed, safe and well.

I felt a great responsibility in this Quest to provide a large and expansive stage to help women process the magnitude of the tragedy. Unlike the Memphis Quest, which occurred while we were all still shell-shocked, this Quest seven weeks after 9/11 called for different resources. Just before the Memphis Quest, I had gone to Grace Cathedral for one of my preparation walks. I wrote the following at the time:

> I stand at the labyrinth in Grace Cathedral a week and a half after the attacks on the World Trade Center. It is a quiet morning. I have the cathedral to myself. I know that the labyrinth has been used frequently in services held over the past days. I step on the path and am immediately assaulted with a feeling of intense grief. I see large, jagged rectangles in my mind's eye and sense fragmentation and distress. It occurs to me that this labyrinth has been the container for abundant grief.

It isn't the first time that I feel I have a relationship with this sacred space and understand that it is the responsibility of those of us who tend the labyrinth to pay attention to its state. I continue my walk, open to receiving guidance about what to bring into the Dream Quest that will be happening in five short weeks. I wonder what the archetypal wise woman would harvest from her spiritual life that might be of use to us all in these difficult times. I have been thinking about the Mother Voice—a voice that seems all too quiet in the climate of war and aggression. As I near the center, I begin to realize that this is a time to call in the most accessible and powerful of the female deities of our cultures. We have spoken the names of the goddesses of all cultures in previous Dream Quests, calling on their significant qualities and enjoying the feminine face of God.

This time, however, I am aware that it is even more important to make a personal relationship with the deities, to let them know that we need their help more than ever. Mary of Christian and Islamic tradition, Tara of the Buddhist, the Shechinah of mystical Judaism, and Kali of Hinduism, the four deities that I mentioned before came swiftly to mind. We would call them, attune ourselves to their aspects, and ask them what to do in this troubled world—ask them how to access the Mother's Voice. A woman portraying the Crone would dance among four women portraying the goddesses and harvest their wisdom. She would inspire the women at the Dream Quest to do the same.

Over the next weeks, I commune with each of the Mothers and ask for her blessing. They answer me at my medicine wheel in the hills behind my home and they answer me in dreams and visions. I read of how Tara comes swiftly when she is called, of how she eschewed enlightenment until she could be enlightened in a woman's body. I remembered how Mary as the Virgin of Guadalupe appeared in my father's hospital room on a poster decrying the disrespectful use of her image declaring "Enough is enough" and stayed in my heart throughout the ordeal of his death. I reread what I could about Kali, a bit frightened of her intensity, but knowing that her fierceness is an essential ingredient of the sacred feminine. I rejoiced in being able to use a beautiful invocation for the Shechinah, which I had set to music, given to me by one of my teachers. Least commonly known, the Shechinah is the indwelling aspect of God, the spiritual essence of all creation. Yes, these Mothers were ready to help. Together, they held the qualities that make up the sacred feminine—they embody devotion; compassion; fierce, unflinching presence; and the ability to permeate all creation. These were definitely the elements of spiritual life that would provide comfort and guidance to the circles of women in these times.

On the night of the Quest, we had a full house. We met each other like long-lost friends, eager to spend time in the beauty of the cathedral and the safety of each other's presence. We sang and walked on the labyrinth. We sighed great sighs of release as we entered the sacred space of our ritual. We greeted each other from our hearts and called the circles of the beloveds, the teachers, and all our relations. Then I asked everyone to sit down and invited the four women who would stand for the Mothers to come forward. They wore intricate black dresses that we had borrowed from the "Women in Black" who keep vigils in the trouble spots on the planet. These dresses had been part of our rituals before. They bear the names of women who have worn them in Jerusalem and Buenos Aires and Santiago and Belfast.

Mary stood in the South for innocence, the Shechinah in the West for depth of inner life, Kali took the wise North, and Tara held the visionary East. I walked to Mary, who was portrayed by a Buddhist woman raised Catholic. All of her sisters have "Mary" as part of their names. I call, "Hail Mary, full of Grace, please be with us. Remind us of the prayers of Christians and Muslims and others who revere you. Teach us your mercy and your constant devotion."

Then I walk to Tara, embodied by a woman who has long chanted her name and meditated with her essence. I call to her, "Buddha in the body of woman, teach us your compassion for all beings." I chant, "Om Tara Tu-tare Tu-re So-ha." Many women join in with the chant—so many of us have been touched with the beauty of this deity.

Next I meet Kali and feel the strong and fearless energy that the woman who portrays her embodies. From 30 years as an Aikido and self-defense instructor, Michelle knows how to channel clarity of purpose and determination. I ask Kali to teach us fierceness and integrity.

Finally I approach the Shechinah. The woman who holds her is a yogini and understands the Shechinah as very much like Shakti, who is the internal energy of the Hindu god, Shiva. The cross-cultural understanding works as she tunes into the power of presence, silent and abiding but ever powerful.

I sing:

> Shechinah, you are the light in my eyes
> Shechinah, you are the breath in my soul
> Shechinah, you are the fire in my blood

> Shechinah, you are the strength in my bones.
>
> You are the love in my heart,
>
> You are the love in my heart.

I am enthralled. I am in right relationship. I feel dizzy as I introduce Thais to stand for us all as she dances with the Mothers, gathering her Crone harvest. As she dances around the circle encountering the deities one by one, she receives a gesture from each one that she takes and makes her own. Just as we encounter a spiritual truth and integrate it into our own being, she portrays the receiving and incorporating ritual of our lives. After she has received the gifts of these gestures, she winds her way back to the center of the circle. The black-veiled deities come toward her and hide her from our view. Inside the embrace of Kali, Tara, Mary, and the Shechinah, Thais then dons a crone mask and an exquisite cape made from an old afghan decorated with bits of cloth and lichen, sticks and bones. She emerges as the crone gifted with the harvest of what she has incorporated from the deities. The Sacred Feminine comes through in the powerful dance. We are filled with this presence; we are hungry for this experience. We have called and have been answered in the land of the soul.

Through this ritual, we make manifest the strength we have to call on in our spiritual lives. We acknowledge that we have partaken of teachings and practices from various traditions and can harvest their wisdom in service of the whole community. Each of the women who enacted the deities felt a strong responsibility to hold the qualities that they manifested and to take seriously what it means to carry these qualities into the world. We suggest that each of us has the power to gather the teachings of our lives through the spiritual traditions that we practice and weave them into a harvest of wisdom. In the small groups, women talked about what they could do to help in the world and the importance of women's voices in the important decisions that were then being made.

Spokane

Spokane is a large city in the high desert of Washington state. In March, the sky was pale blue. Spring had not yet touched the hills with green, and buds were tight on their branches. I had left the very green hills of a California spring watered by the storms that usually drench the Northwest. Spokane looked thirsty, caught on the dry side of global warming.

Kathy has invited me and the Dream Quest to come to Spokane based on her intuition. Her Episcopal congregation is conservative, in the midst of a very poor and blighted region. There are huge SUVs and junker cars, dilapidated housing next to the once-proud Victorians. Downtown has been "saved" by a mall featuring Nordstrom's, Pottery Barn, and the usual suspects. There are signs around the cathedral that say that one in three people in

Spokane are affected by domestic violence, listing numbers to call for help. My hostess says the domestic violence is the result of the poverty—no mines to work in, the Boeing plant closed, the military base curtailed, the timber industry dried up. There is a lot of meth use, she says. People are desperately poor.

On the night before the Quest, I stay in the house of one of the women who will be participating. She is in her 70s and leaves me alone because she needs to drive thirty miles each day to stay with her grandchildren overnight. The parents work opposing shifts, and there is a time no one is home in the early morning hours. She leaves me her bed with crisp white sheets. There is a deep sadness in this house—chock full of projects and the accumulation of many years. I am not surprised to find out that her divorce will be final the next week. "None too soon," she says.

Kathy has a handicapped sticker on her car. She is enormous, and laughs about it. Her knees are arthritic. She works at the state hospital and has hopes of finishing her B.A. and becoming a deacon or a priest. She is sharp and funny. We laugh at the horrors of George Bush's America and praise Molly Ivins.

When I awake in the morning, I walk out into the park. It is clear that this was once a fine neighborhood. Large, now-shabby homes surround this park full of pine and deciduous trees still in the grip of winter. I pick twigs with tiny emerging leaves and a branch that is greening. I am reminded of the meaning of our sponsor's name, "Veriditas": the Greening Power of God. Kathy drives me around the river area where old hippies live in interesting houses. We pass the huge Victorian mansions of the industrial age.

At last we arrive at the cathedral, which seems to have been dropped out of time and space from 13th century England. It sits on a hill up from the river with a high tower and cruciform design. It is a jewel, meticulously created by a famous early 20th century architect who was a 3rd degree Mason. Financed by the wealth of an earlier era, it is a splendid recreation of the old cathedrals that I have seen in England without the wear and tear of the ages. Each nook and cranny is painstakingly created: carved stone, jewel-colored stained glass windows, richly embroidered kneeling cushions. Sacred geometry creates the same feeling, whether here or in medieval European cathedrals.

The canvas labyrinth that we will use during the Quest is in the north transept. It is worn, with candle wax spills and stains. Because it is smaller than the labyrinths I am used to, it feels squeezed into a corner here, a product of its time and circumstances in stark contrast to the grand creation of an earlier, more prosperous era.

I meet with the small group leaders, all church women, though two of the women have been to trainings in California and are more comfortable with an ecumenical format. I think of all the other circles that I have led in different parts of the country. I trust the power of the exercises that have brought these other circles to a place of calm. I take the group leaders through breathing exercises and the Circles Meditation, and suggest that they use prayer to discover what they hope to experience during this Quest. They comply and then share stories about their lives, several with tears. They seem thirsty, like the hills. And they seem a bit bewildered about this obviously different way of working.

We arrange the space, moving chairs right into the quire, the central power point of the cathedral. The small group leaders make their altars, which they want to place high on tabletops instead of on the floor, like we do at Grace. Everything is new to them and probably a bit frightening, though no one voices this. Soon we walk the labyrinth together, something that always builds the energy in San Francisco. I feel as though I need to keep gathering up the energy. We have a beautiful dinner on fine china in the church dining hall. Then it is time for the Quest.

The participants are slow in coming and the space seems to be too large for us. Finally enough of us gather to begin the singing. It will be a small group, just under thirty. There is something about standing in this space that has been the province of the patriarchal clergy throughout all the ages, in this distressed city that moves me deeply. Being here where so much about the American Dream has gone wrong and choosing to sing to the Divine Mother is simply revolutionary. As we sing I wait for the "lifting up" that unfailingly occurs at the Quest. This time it feels like lifting a giant resistant octopus. But then something wonderful begins to happen.

The women enter the labyrinth singing "Return Again." I hear the tentative voices begin to strengthen and harmonize. During the Greeting Dance, tears start to flow. Nearly everyone is crying. We call the circles and then we light large votive candles and walk in procession up the main aisle singing "Dona Nobis Pacem." It is a song that many women know and the harmonies begin to fill the space. We place the candles on the altar for the night. They are a light in the darkness of the tall cathedral—a statement of our presence that fills the space with the energy of the sacred feminine. Small groups start working together and the sound of conversation and laughter echoes throughout the cathedral. Women begin to relax, and I begin to trust that whatever is meant to happen will happen.

Later in the evening, I offer healings to individual women. Two women come who have had cancer, one is still in treatment. They drink in the Reiki and the conversation. I also receive a healing from two women who anoint me and pray with me, asking the Holy Spirit for blessings. I feel the similarity between my Reiki work and this traditional practice of the laying on of hands. By the end of the Quest, we have bonded. I am invited back for a second year.

Galveston

Like Spokane and Memphis, Galveston, Texas, is in a part of the country I wouldn't think of as a likely place for a Quest. And like the response at those other venues, the success of the Quest here is a heartening experience. I am continually amazed that women are willing to leave their individual doctrines and beliefs at the cathedral door and to drop down into the essentials of their gender for seventeen hours. During that time they achieve points of insight into their individual lives and more clearly define their hopes and dreams for their families, their nation, and the whole of humanity. I know that we have hit upon a formula for inviting just the right mixture of reflection, humor, and a serious understanding of the troubles of the world. Part of that "formula" is to be flexible and creative. We temper the traditions of the Quest with an ever-changing influx of seasonal practices and ideas based on current events and the needs of the culture of a particular place. Here is how the Quest evolved in Galveston.

In January 2003, while attending a Veriditas reunion, I met Dr. Kay Sandor, who was involved with the Labyrinth Project at William Temple Center in Galveston. Kay was researching the effects of labyrinth walking on people's stress levels. She led full-moon walks and tended the beautiful garden that surrounded the labyrinth. I made a short presentation on the Quest and she was intrigued. How would I like to come to Galveston, she asked? Well,

I said, I was scheduled to go to Houston next fall and maybe could come to Galveston as well.

As we got closer to the time of the Quest, there was some concern about using the Native American medicine cards in this setting. Perhaps we needed to use more neutral or Christian imagery to choose the themes for our small groups. Since the leader of the center did not know me and had never attended a Quest, I thought this was a reasonable request. I gave her a set of qualities that we had used at a Quest called the Daughters of the Divine Mother: compassion, wisdom, nurture, receptivity, protection, unconditional love, and loyalty.

When I arrived, our host Rev. Posy was picking bouquets for the dinner tables. Her assistant was hard at work on three soups and a chicken salad. I was welcomed with open arms and told about a spirit who seemed to haunt the center. They told me the ghost was friendly and that I was not to worry about being harmed in any way. I began to think that our world views were not as different as I had surmised.

Soon the local small group leaders began to arrive. They seemed so open-minded to all types of spirituality they could have been the same women who come to Portland or San Francisco. They wore the same flowing outfits and welcomed each other with loving respect. My California prejudices about women's spirituality in the heartland were rightly challenged and vanquished.

I began our meeting with a long guided meditation that took the small group leaders into the places in their bodies that called to them, asking them to listen to the messages they heard. Then I asked them to imagine the circles in their lives—their beloved ones, the ones who gave them spiritual succor, the circle of all beings with whom we share the planet. They went into the meditation as individuals and came out a circle, chatting and joking with each other. They had a lot to say about the qualities they had received as the focal theme of their small groups. One woman, who was in the middle of a divorce, received "loyalty." Another woman got "receptivity," which made her wonder if she had been too receptive for far too long. We had a lively discussion as we got to know each other, exploring how these qualities impacted us; surprisingly, it was the same sort of discussion we would have had if we had been talking about the archetypes invoked by the images on the animal cards I usually use. The leaders were all happy to be part of a larger circle of women doing similar work. I spoke of my desire to create circles like this all over the country. They nodded, understanding a common longing to find our way to a more powerful and visible presence in the world.

As it turned out, the enrollment was not what had been anticipated, and it was necessary for two leaders to tend each group. During a quick and fairly random selection process, receptivity went with protection, wisdom with loyalty, and compassion with nurture. Unconditional love stood alone. The conversations in the small groups were very rich and fruitful. The group leaders each appreciated having another leader to work with, and much of the work of building the circle was complete. I thought that this might be a model for the future, having two leaders immediately softens the notion of hierarchy. The interplay between the two qualities in each group also guaranteed discussion at a different level. For example, the loyalty/wisdom group decided collectively that loyalty to oneself was the precursor to wisdom.

With a nod to Southern hospitality, the participants were offered a delicious dinner as they arrived. Afterward we moved the tables away to make way for the labyrinth, which was painted onto a large canvas. Candles were brought out and the lights dimmed. We circled up and began to sing. Just as women had done in the cathedrals of San Francisco and Portland, the participants made their way onto the labyrinth singing "Return Again" and the magic that always attends the Quest settled in. We called on our inner Maiden, Mother and Crone. Then I invoked the circles of beloveds, ancestors and deities, reminding the Galveston women that other women had stood in these circles before them and sung the same songs, greeted each other in the same way and come together with the same intentions for personal and planetary healing. We imagined this circle joining with the other circles. Yes, I thought, every circle has a place and the more circles we create, the less likely we will be to see each other as across the divide of red and blue states. When we relate to one another as our innocent maiden selves and are invited to see that same vulnerability mirrored in the others around us, we are able to let go of so many beliefs that separate us. The here and now of this moment of relationship is what becomes important. We see the common humanity in the circle and relax into a shared experience.

After we had created our circle inside the building, we each lit a candle and walked in silence into the balmy night air to a garden labyrinth planted with sage and lavender. Insects chirped and the traffic noises faded into the background as we walked together, a new circle of women moving into the land of the soul.

The 20th Anniversary in Grace

On the 20th anniversary of the Quest, along with our usual participants, we invited two babies, several young maidens, and an 86-year-old woman who had seen Grace Cathedral being built some 60 years ago. Our theme was "Dreaming the Way Home." After so many years of being in the cathedral, many of us remarked about how much it had become a kind of home for us. Having the whole spectrum of womanhood present made the cathedral feel like an archetypal village.

We built an altar near the labyrinth that contained the elements of our Gaia Home—a fountain representing water, stones representing the earth, candles representing fire, and feathers representing the air. Each of the participants brought something from their own homes to add to the collective altar. There were photos of family, a teddy bear, a coffee mug, precious rocks and crystals, and statues.

We contemplated what it means to be at home inside of ourselves, with our families, our communities, and our planet. Being at home is the opposite of being alienated and isolated. Being at home is belonging. When we are home in our bodies, our breath flows unimpeded and carries life force to every cell. When we are at home in our houses, we can find sanctuary from the difficulties of the world and create beauty that soothes the soul. When we are at home in the community, we feel a part of the collective, more naturally responsive to the needs of others. When we are at home on our Earth, we are naturally inclined toward conservation and preservation. We are able to feel a kinship to the whole of creation. The first step is creating a sense of home in ourselves. By doing so, we suggest that this "homing" is something we can cultivate in the world.

In order to find home inside ourselves, we begin with the breath and notice the place in our bodies that draws our attention when we think of our center. Often this is our heart, although many people feel most centered in their spines or bellies. There is no right or wrong place. What is useful is to have a dependable place to refer to in the body. Then when we feel scattered or confused, we can use the breath to come "home." After establishing this sense of home in our initial exercises, we used our ritual to identify several archetypes qualities that enhance our spiritual home.

We settled on invoking The Holy Spirit, The Mother, The Crone, The Warrior, and The Circle. We asked different women to portray these archetypes through costume and dance, and used chanting to call them into the circle. As a group, we chanted, "Veni Sancte Spiritus," which means, "Come, Holy Spirit," as a drone while Joan's beautiful soprano voice sang these words:

> Come Holy Spirit
> Fill us with your love
> Take us home to our hearts
> With your sweet grace
>
> Come holy Mother
> Hold us in your arms
> Take us home to your safety
> Free from harm
>
> Come holy Crone
> Show us courage and ease
> Take us home to your hearth
> and teach us peace

Come holy warrior
Teach us, each, our part
Save our Gaia Home
And every heart

Come holy circle
Hear our hopes and our fears
Take us home to the trust
Of love so dear

As Joan called in the Holy Spirit, Tenaya, the only 8-year-old who has been coming to the Quest since she was in her mother's womb, came running down the central aisle from the high altar to the labyrinth, trailing five dozen rainbow-colored nylon scarves tied end to end in her wake. She came to the center of the labyrinth and I covered her with the scarves to depict the fact that sometimes the spirit becomes hidden from view. Next, Joan called the Mother, and Ann and Karen brought their babies into the circle. The Mother is essential in our sense of home. Then, Joan invited the Crone into our midst and Clover appeared from behind the veils wearing the Crone mask and walking with a crooked stick. We need wisdom and experience to create Home.

The next element of our ceremony came because of Thais's

dream. During the time when she had been creating a dance to depict the theme of Home, she dreamed that the element of protection was essential in our creation of Home. So she carried a sword and wore her beautiful kimono emblazoned with a tiger while she danced to remind us of the fierce compassion necessary to protect our internal and external homes. The warrior archetype is essential when considering the protection of our Gaia Home.

In her dance, Thais released her daughter, Tenaya, from the pile of scarves and unwound them, handing them to the women in the circle. Then Tenaya herself danced, her young exuberant movement releasing spirit into our midst.

Once the circle had been formed, we brought back the babies and sang a lullaby accompanied by Diana's harp. Next we welcomed two maidens who were coming to the Quest for the first time following their first blood. Thais put the ends of the scarves into the maidens' hands and they led us all from the labyrinth to the Home Altar. In this dance, accompanied by harp music, we encircled the elemental Home Altar and then wound our way back to the labyrinth.

That year like many others, Cindy Pavlinak, extraordinary Sacred Sites photographer shared a slideshow of her images depicting Home and the sacred feminine. Images of ancient stone circles, labyrinths, and portraits of female deities were projected onto silk veils hung from the mezzanine. The images floated, enormous above us. That night many women sat by the Home altar, watching the images and contemplating how to create home in their hearts, their families and their lives.

These are only some of the Quests that have occurred over these 25 years. Each one is like a unique and beautiful bead strung on a cord of common songs and practices. Each Quest has nourished and challenged a group of women to enter into the land of the soul and to embrace the gifts of the sacred feminine. It is my hope that they will continue to do so, adapting to different places and times.

Chapter Ten
Growing the Vision

Circle by circle we grow

Ten

As I look at *Sisiutl*, the piece that graces the cover of this book, I see a depiction of the Quest. The canoe that takes the maiden, mother, and crone across the waters has a mythological animal on its bow, a sea creature who, according to the Kwakiutl people of the Pacific Northwest, has the power to go between the worlds and provide safe passage to the land of the soul. I hope that the Quest is such a canoe, plying the emotional waters of ordinary life in search of an entrance to the spiritual realms, taking all aspects of ourselves along for the ride. In the Quest we harken back to ancient ways of knowing and gathering. We are like an Indian council or a Pagan ceremony honoring the seasons. We are like a medieval Christian pilgrimage seeking the holy land in the middle of the labyrinth, and we are a modern-day support group that recognizes the power of sharing the joys and sorrows of our lives. We are women recognizing the beauty of the feminine face of God. We are weavers of ancient and modern ways. We are weavers of the strands of many religions and cultures. We meet in the circle to honor all of the ways human beings meet the sacred. We quest a circle way of community and spirit.

Just before I completed this manuscript, I met with my writing group, faithful companions during the process of bringing 25 years of candlelit labyrinth walks, powerful ritual circles, oceans of tears, and moments of pure joy and unitive consciousness to the printed page. I came to my friends worrying that this wasn't a perfect creation, afraid that it wouldn't depict the Quest as I have come to know and love it. They looked at me with their wise eyes, knowing me, this work, and the creative process and advised me to let this book be born, have a life of its own, and let go of the outcome. Truly that kind of trust in Life has been at the core of my creation of the Quest during all of these years. That trust is the secret loving ingredient that creates the magic. These words come from that trust and it is my prayer that you have been aided in your own Quest in the land of the soul.

My high hopes for the future of the Quest is reflected in the Circles Meditation. I see a series of concentric circles rippling out into the world. I see Quests and the circles that they encourage thriving in diverse communities. I see the Quest as a refuge for the sacred feminine, a dependable gathering place for women and a yearly reminder of the power of the circle. Every time I have told women in a new location that circles of women in San Francisco or Portland have been doing the Quest for decades, they sigh and smile, knowing that they now belong to a larger circle of women who understand the need to come together to harvest their wisdom and celebrate the sacred feminine. When we know that other women in other places are having similar experiences, we sense inclusion and power, and dream of the possibilities bringing change to the world. Singing the same songs and enjoying the same practices creates a sense of belonging to a larger sisterhood. I believe like Jean Shinoda Bolen suggests, when we reach the millionth circle, our world will be a fundamentally different place.

After 25 years of Quests in San Francisco and 12 years in Portland, I see the fruits of yearly gathering. Deep friendships are forged and the gifts of community—support in times of need, reliable witness to transitions and celebrations of all kinds, projects of service and reflection—are tangible. I have learned to be patient, waiting until just the right people appear to take leadership in their communities. This is only one impulse toward the soulful life in a world of many possibilities. I hope that more communities will receive the Quest and that the circles spread.

The Quest represents a post-modern reflection of an ancient, indigenous way of soulful celebration that is rising up from the belly of the beast of our fractionalized, consumer culture. I always trust that, given half a chance a group of modern women will instinctively know how to circle up, breathe deeply, and quiet their minds. They will remember the power of collective prayer to benefit our families, our friends, our communities, and our own dear hearts. I believe that this remembering of the circle is latent in our consciousness. Along with the archetypes of the labyrinth, the land of the soul, the Maiden, the Mother, and the Crone, remembering the circle ignites an experience of the deeper levels in our collective consciousness. The movement of breath, the circle dances, the candle light, the simple rituals and songs—all of these things soothe our frenzied modern minds and return us to the land of the soul. And when we arrive in that land, we relax, we have room to dream and room to make choices about how to live. We remember how to find the personal and collective will to heal and change.

Along with Ferron's song, I pray that:

> By my life, be I spirit,
>
> By my heart, be I woman
>
> By my eyes, be I open
>
> And by my hands, be I whole.

The Songs

Every song that a human sings
with his or her voice is
only an expression
of that One Great Song
that is there from the beginning
and will be there after the end.

                                      Brother David Steindl Rast

Return Again

By Schlomo Carlbach

Earth My Body

By Ferron

Deep Peace

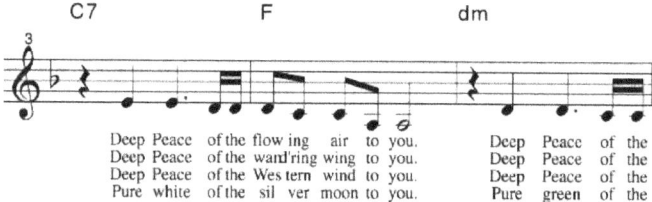
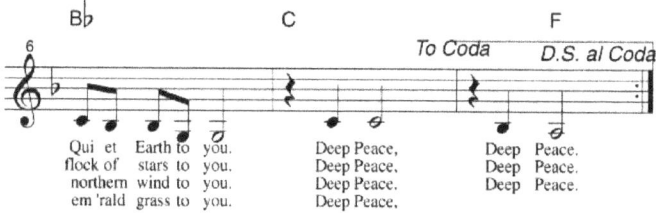
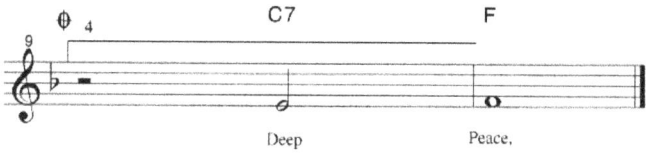

Divine Mother

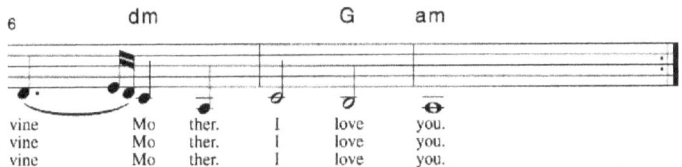

Mother I Sing To You

Judith Tripp

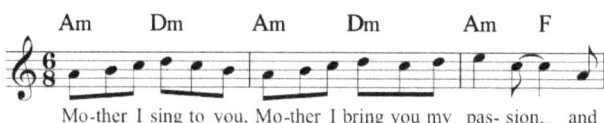
Mo-ther I sing to you, Mo-ther I bring you my pas- sion, and

pre- sence. Mo-ther I sing to you, Mo-ther I give you my life.

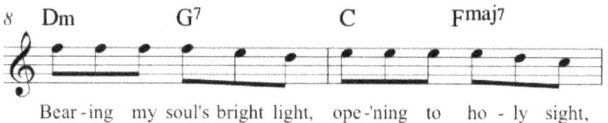
Bear-ing my soul's bright light, ope-'ning to ho - ly sight,

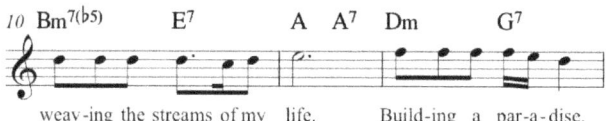
weav-ing the streams of my life. Build-ing a par-a-dise,

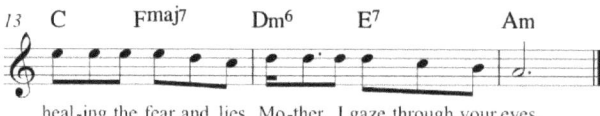
heal-ing the fear and lies, Mo-ther I gaze through your eyes.

Circle of Wisdom

Judith Tripp

continued

203

Circle of Wisdom, continued

The circle will hold you, our arms will embrace you
Your joys and sufferings shared.
You'll give us your wisdom, the harvest of living,
We'll celebrate knowing you're here.

Our times are calling all people of wisdom
Who love our Earth and her kin,
It's time to take our place in the circle
And let the healing begin.

The Well Song

Irish Blessing Dance

Resources

Books:

Artress, Lauren, *Walking a Sacred Path*, 1996
Baldwin, Christina, *Calling the Circle*, 1994
Bloom, Ralph, The Book of Runes, 1982
Bolen, Jean Shinoda, *The Millionth Circle*, 1999
Geoffrion, Jill, *Praying the Chartres Labyrinth*, 2006
O'Donohue, John, *To Bless the Space Between Us*, 2008
Oliver, Mary, *White Iris*, 2004
Sams, Jamie, *The Medicine Cards*, 1988

Visuals:

Cindy A. Pavlinak, Sacred Land Photography,
http://www.sacred-land-photography.com

Music:

Diana Stork, harp music and CDs,
www.harpdancer.com
Portia Diwa, harp music and CDs,
www.portiadiwa.com

About Circleway

Circleway, www.Circleway.com, is a collection of enterprises that include the Women's Dream Quest, Pilgrimages to Avalon, Individual Psychotherapy, and an online store where you can purchase CDs and books.

Avalon

Judith leads a yearly Pilgrimage to Avalon, a six-day journey to the sacred sites of Southwest England, including Glastonbury, Stonehenge, Avebury, and Tintagel on the Cornwall coast. We stay in a retreat center in Glastonbury and explore the inner and outer landscape of megalithic, Arthurian, and modern-day Avalon.

CDs

homage, solo flute in Celtic Sacred Sites, recorded live on location in England and France

Return Again, Songs from the Women's Dream Quest featuring the songs mentioned in this book

To Bless the Walk, Solo Flute on the Chartres Labyrinth, recorded live at a Veriditas-sponsored Labyrinth walk at Chartres Cathedral, France

Hosting a Dream Quest in Your Area

Judith is available to create a Quest for your community. She works with the overnight format described in this book and also with daylong and weekend time frames. Please contact her at Judith@circleway.com for further information. She will supply you with *The Dream Quest Planner* which outlines everything you need to know to produce a Dream Quest, as well as telephone consultations, training for small group leaders and leadership and music on the day of the Quest.

It is helpful to have access to a labyrinth although we can create one on site. You will need a large room, several facilitators trained in group dynamics, and a circle of women to help advertise, organize, and dream. While most Quests have been held in large churches, they have also been held outdoors, in gymnasiums, and at retreat centers. Please call Judith at 415.552.4546 if you have questions about adapting the Quest to your particular circumstances.

Acknowledgments

I want to acknowledge all of the women who have come to Quests over the years. Thank you for receiving this work. And thank you from the bottom of my heart to the small group leaders in San Francisco and around the country who give of their hearts and souls to each Quest. You are the circle that holds me.

I have great gratitude for my writing group, Francis Weller, Michelle Keip, and Astrid Berg who have nurtured every word I have written and kept me faithful to my task.

Thank you to my excellent and inspirational editor, Joy Parker, who has gently nudged me into fuller expression and good story telling.

And thank you to Lauren Artress, the founder of Veriditas, our sponsor. Through your friendship and trust, you have made the space for my work to unfold. And to Dawn Matheny and the rest of the Veriditas staff, board and council for your support.

To Crystal Forthomme, who co-facilitated the Quest in San Francisco for many years, I offer my lifelong love. And to Gyllian Davies, Peg Edera, Leia Durland Jones, and the other brave women who have brought the Quest to their home ground, I thank you for the enduring friendships that we have formed.

To Diana Stork, Portia Diwa, Cindy Pavlinak, Joan Curry, Kayleen Asbo, and Thais and Tenaya Mazur, I offer my gratitude for the artistry you have generously contributed over the years.

To Jacob Barnett, I offer my appreciation for computer acumen and great design ideas.

To Laura Cucullu, I offer gratitude for her eagle eyes and midwifery.

And of course to my star, Gwyneth Tripp, who designed the cover and helps her mother create in every way.

www.ingramcontent.com/pod-product-compliance
Lightning Source LLC
Chambersburg PA
CBHW032110090426
42743CB00007B/308